PICTURE DICTIONARY

ENGLISH

ENGLISH PICTURE DICTIONARY

Copyright © 1990 Éditions Rényi Inc.

Illustrated by Kathryn Adams, Pat Gangnon, Colin Gillies, David Shaw and Yvonne Zan.
Designed by David Shaw and Associates.

Typesetting by Osgoode Technical Translations

Color separations by New Concept Limited

Printed in Canada by Metropole Litho Inc.

Edited by K. L. Cordner, P. O'Brien-Hitching, R. LeBel, P. Rényi.

Originally published by Éditions Rényi Inc., Toronto, Canada

Distributed exclusively in trade and education in the United States of America by Langenscheidt Publishers, Inc., Maspeth, New York 11378

Hardcover	ISBN 0-88729-850-8
Softcover	ISBN 0-88729-856-7

Distributed outside the USA by Éditions Rényi Inc., Toronto, Canada

Hardcover	ISBN 0-921606-00-1
Softcover	ISBN 0-921606-46-X

INTRODUCTION

Some of Canada's best illustrators have contributed to this Picture Dictionary, which has been carefully designed to combine words and pictures into a pleasurable learning experience.

Its unusually large number of terms (3336) makes this Picture Dictionary a flexible teaching tool. It is excellent for helping young children acquire language and dictionary skills. Because the vocabulary it encompasses is so broad, this dictionary can also be used to teach new words to older children and adults as well. Further, it is also an effective tool for teaching English as a second language.

THE VOCABULARY

The decision on which words to include and which to leave out was made in relation to three standards. First, a word-frequency analysis was carried out to include the most common words. Then a thematic clustering analysis was done to make sure that words in common themes (animals, plants, activities etc.) were included. Finally, the vocabulary was expanded to include words which children would likely hear, ask about and use. This makes this dictionary's vocabulary more honest than most. 'To choke', 'greedy', 'to smoke' are included, but approval is withheld.

This process was further complicated by the decision to *systematically* illustrate the meanings. Although the degree of abstraction was kept reasonably low, it was considered necessary to include terms such as 'to expect' and 'to forgive', which are virtually impossible to illustrate. Instead of dropping these terms, we decided to provide explanatory sentences that create a context.

Where variations occur between British and North American English, both terms are given, with an asterisk marking the British version (favor/favour*, gas/petrol*).

USING THIS DICTIONARY

Used at home, this dictionary is an enjoyable book for children to explore alone or with their parents. The pictures excite the imagination of younger children and entice them to ask questions. Older children in televisual cultures often look to visual imagery as an aid to meaning. The pictures help them make the transition from the graphic to the written. Even young adults will find the book useful, because the illustrations, while amusing, are not childish.

The dictionary as a whole provides an occasion to introduce students to basic dictionary skills. This work is compatible with school reading materials in current use, and can serve as a 'user-friendly' reference tool.

Great care has been taken to ensure that any contextual statements made are factual, have some educational value and are compatible with statements made elsewhere in the book. Lastly, from a strictly pedagogical viewpoint, the little girl featured in the book has not been made into a paragon of virtue; young users will readily identify with her imperfections.

TO MY NEW FRIENDS

My name is Ashley. I am a little girl. I go to school, I am learning to swim, I have a little brother and many, many ideas. If you want to meet my father, the admiral, look at the page on the right. You will see him at the bottom of the page. My mother is on the next page, at the top. If you want to meet me, look up the word "calm".

Some people think dictionaries are dull. I guess they have not seen this one, which is all about me and the people I know.

Five grown-up illustrators had a lot of fun drawing the pictures. I also drew a picture (the zebra). Can you find it?

I must go now. Look for me in the dictionary.

Ashley

P.S. If you want to write to me about our dictionary, ask your parents or your teacher for my address.

1   abacus

2   about
Tell me **about** it.
It takes **about** an hour.
Jack went **about** his work.

3   above
The apple is **above** her head.

4   absent
Paul is **absent** today.

5   accelerator
Every car has an **accelerator**.

6   accent
Jacques speaks with a French **accent**.
Put the **accent** on the first syllable.

7   accident

8   accordion

9   to accuse
They all **accused** Nancy.

10   ace
The **ace** of spades

11   My head **aches**.

12   acid
Acid can burn your skin.

13   acorn
Oak trees grow from **acorns**.

14   acrobat

15   across
Paul lives **across** the road.
He came **across** an old friend yesterday.

16   to add
Add them together.

17   address
This is Ashley's **address**.

18   admiral
Ashley's father is an **admiral**.

19   to adore
I **adore** you.

Adults are grown-ups.

20   adult

Advance your king.

21   to advance

Is it an **advantage** to be tall?

22   advantage

Ashley's mum loves **adventure**.

23   adventure

24   He is **afraid**..

Africa is a continent.

25   Africa

You can play **after** dinner.

Repeat **after** me!

Run **after** the ball!

26   after

Afternoon starts at 12 o'clock.

27   afternoon

Play it **again**, Sam!

Then **again,** you could play something different…

28   again

Tigger rubs **against** Jim's leg.

29   to rub **against**

What a difference in **age**!

30   age

Athletes are very **agile**.

31   agile person

32   aground

Reg is going **ahead** with his plans.

Plan **ahead** for your next holiday.

Helen is **ahead** of Jane in reading.

33   ahead

34   to provide **aid**

Is she **aiming** straight?

35   to aim

The kite is flying in the **air**.

36   air

37   air mattress

Insect in an **airtight** container

38   airtight

This **aeroplane** seems to be in trouble.

39   airplane/aeroplane*

Planes land at the **airport**.	You can walk down the **aisle**.		A photo **album**
40 airport	41 aisle	42 alarm clock	43 album
The house is **alight**!	One fish is definitely **alive**.		A cat in the back **alley**
44 alight	45 alive	46 I want them **all**.	47 alley
		Spot can **almost** reach the bone.	Why is he sitting **alone**?
48 alligator	49 almond	50 almost	51 alone
Come **along** with me!		A B C D E F G H I J K L M N O P Q R S T U V W X Y Z a b c d e f g h i j k l m n o p q r s t u v w x y z	
52 along	53 aloud	54 alphabet	55 Do I have to go **already**?
It hurts, but I am **alright**.			You should **always** be careful.
56 I am **alright**.	57 I **also** want some.	58 aluminum/aluminium* ladder	59 I **always** fall down.

60 ambulance

61 wolf **among** sheep

62 anchor

Ancient ruins

63 ancient

64 angle

Why is Spud **angry**?

65 He is **angry**.

66 **animals**

67 ankle

Mark **announces** the start of the race.

68 to **announce**

69 **another** sandwich

70 The **answer** is…

71 ant

72 Antarctic

73 antelope

74 antlers

75 I do not have **any** money.

76 It eats **anything**.

Spud is angry because…

77 He cannot go **anywhere**.

One is **apart** from the bunch.

78 apart

79 ape

80 apiary	81 to apologize/apologise*	82 to appear	83 to applaud
84 apple	85 apple core	86 to approach	87 apricot
88 April	89 apron	90 aquarium	91 arch
92 architect	93 Arctic	94 to argue	95 arm
96 armchair	97 armor/armour*	98 armpit	99 around

To **apologise** means to say you are sorry.

I **apologise** for being late!

He **appeared** out of nowhere.

It **appears** to be snowing.

The Queen **appeared** on television.

April showers bring May flowers.

It is very cold in the **Arctic**.

Sir Galahad wears **armour**.

Around the world in eighty days

The lake is all **around** us.

100   to **arrange** flowers

The police **arrested** Spud.

101   to **arrest**

102   to **arrive**

103   arrow

104   artichoke

Clare wants to become an **artist**.

105   artist

As soon **as** you like.

As for you, I think you are in trouble!

As pretty **as** a picture

106   as

107   ash

108   ashtray

Asia is a continent.

109   Asia

110 to **ask** for directions

Mary and Fluffy are both sound **asleep**.

111   asleep

112   asparagus

Two **aspirins** might help.

113   aspirin

Gary has **astonished** Jane.

114   to **astonish**

115   astronaut

116   astronomer

Helen is **at** home with her dad.

They are looking **at** the picture.

Go to bed **at** once!

117   at

118   athlete

Can you find your country in this **atlas**?

119   atlas

120 atmosphere
The **atmosphere** of the Earth

121 atom

122 to **attach**

123 Pay **attention!**

124 **attic**
What do you store in the **attic?**

125 **audience**

126 **August**
August is the eighth month of the year.

127 My **aunt** is my mother's sister.

128 **Australia**
Australia is an island continent.

129 **author**

130 **automatic**
An **automatic** awakening

131 **autumn**
Autumn is one of the four seasons.

132 **avalanche**

133 **avocado**

134 **awake**
Why is Spud wide **awake?**

135 She is **away.**

136 an **awful** smell

137 an **awkward** person

138 **axe**

139 **axle**
The **axle** links two wheels.

B

Babies are cute!

140   baby

141   baby carriage/pram*

Scratch my **back**!

142   back

144   **bacon** and eggs

145   **bad** apple

146   badge

143   to back up

What is inside the **bag**?

147   bag

The **bait** attracts the mouse.

148   bait

149   to bake

150   baker

151   bakery

152   good **balance**

153   balcony

Tom is **bald**.

154   bald

155   ball

156   ballerina

157   ballet

158   balloon

159 hot air **balloon**

160 banana

This **band** is a headband.

161 band

162 musical **band**

A **bandage** made it feel better.

163 bandage

164 to bang

Sliding down the **banister**

165 banister

Do you have a **bank** account?

166 bank

167 bar

Pubs are for adults!

168 bar/pub*

169 barbed wire

The **barber** cuts Michael's hair.

170 barber

171 one **bare** foot

A **bargain** at this price

172 bargain

Barges travel along the canals.

173 barge

174 to bark

Barley is grown on the farm.

176 barley

177 barn

Soldiers live in **barracks.**

178 barracks

175 bark

A **barrel** of olive oil
179 barrel

The **barrel** of a gun
180 barrel

181 barrette/hair slide*

182 barrier

The **base** of a column
183 base

A baseball **base**
184 base

185 baseball

186 basement/cellar*

187 basil

188 basket

189 basketball

A baseball **bat**
190 bats

192 I am having a **bath**.

193 bathroom

194 bathtub

Bats fly at night.
191 bat

A **battery** for your radio
195 battery

196 bay

Mother uses **bay leaves** for cooking.
197 bay leaves

198 bazaar

Do you promise to **be** good?

I **am** good.

Tom and Bob **are** good, but **is** Ashley good?

199   to **be**

200   beach

A whole string of **beads**

201   bead

202   beak

203   **beam** of light

204   beans

Billy the **bear** can ride a bicycle.

205   bear

A long **beard**

206   beard

What an awful-looking **beast**!

207   beast

Nellie **beats** the drum.

208   to **beat**

209   beautiful

Beavers build dams.

210   beaver

...I lost my cat.

211   I am crying **because**...

212   to **become**

213   bed

214 bed lamp/reading light*

215   bedroom

The **bee** is a useful insect.

216   bee

217   beech

Bees live in **beehives**.

218   beehive

A mug of **beer**	**Beetroot** grows in the ground.		
219 beer	220 beet/beetroot*	221 beetle	222 Wash your hands **before** dinner.

To **begin** with, let's have breakfast!

Ashley's piano lesson **begins** at ten o'clock.

Our piano lesson **begins** at nine o'clock.

Alice **behaves** well.

Julia hides **behind** the tree.

223 to beg	224 to begin	225 to behave	226 behind
227 beige	228 I **believe** in dragons.	229 bell	230 belly button

The cat is **below** the table.

231 He **belongs** to me.	232 below	233 belt	234 bench

A **bend** in the road

Pat stands **beside** the tree.

235 bend	236 to bend	237 beret	238 beside

Should you not eat something else **besides** dessert?

Besides, you should not eat so much sugar.

239   besides

240   best

Sheila writes **better** than Tom.

Tom is lazy, he can do **better.**

241   better

Phil walks **between** the rocks.

242   between

243   bib

244   bicycle

245   big

A **bike** is a bicycle.

246   bike

247   bill/banknote*

248   billboard/hoarding*

Snooker is a game.

249   billiards/snooker*

250   to bind/tie up*

251   binoculars

252   bird

Ashley weighed seven pounds at **birth.**

The **birth** of a nation

The cat gave **birth** to four little kittens.

253   birth

Happy **birthday** to you!

254   birthday

255   biscuit

Fred **bites** into his sandwich.

256   to bite

He took a big **bite.**

257   bite

Beer has a **bitter** taste.

Ashley wept **bitter** tears when she lost her favourite doll.

258   bitter

259   black

260   blackberry

There are many species of **blackbird**.

261   blackbird

Colin drew this on the **blackboard**.

262   blackboard

263   blackcurrant

264   blacksmith

The **blade** is sharp!

265   blade

Father **blamed** Ashley, but she did not do it.

Father should **blame** Crispin, who did do it!

266   to **blame**

267   **blank** page

268   blanket

A **blast** is an explosion.

269   blast

270   to **blast**

The firefighters put out the **blaze**.

271   blaze

272   blazer

Bleach helps clean the laundry.

273   bleach

Her nose is **bleeding**.

274   to **bleed**

275   blender

The **blind** cannot see.

276   blind

277   to **blink**

Blisters hurt!

278   blister

279   blizzard

Do you play with **blocks**?

280   block

The car is going round the **block**.

281   block

The policeman **blocks** John's way.

282   to block

Blonde hair

283   blond/blonde*

A **blood** transfusion

284   blood

The flower is in full **bloom**.

285   bloom

286   to blossom

An ink **blot**

287   blot

288   blouse

289   a **blow** to the head

290   to blow

291   blue

292   blueberries

This knife is too **blunt** to cut the tomato.

Sometimes it is better to be **blunt** when giving your friend the bad news.

293   blunt

Cora **blushes** easily.

294   to blush

295   boar

296   board

Christopher likes to **boast**.

His modesty is nothing to **boast** about.

297   to boast

298   boat

299   bobby pin/hairgrip*

The human **body**

300   body

301   to **boil**

302   bolt

A **bone** for the dog

303   bone

304   bonfire

305   book

306   bookshelf

307   boomerang

308   boot

Border between two countries

309   border

It is hard to **bore** a hole in concrete.

310   to **bore**

What year were you **born**?

She is a **born** leader.

312   born

Can I **borrow** some money?

Ashley often **borrows** her brother's bike.

313   to **borrow**

314   boss

Ashley can **bore** people to death.

Bob **bores** me because he talks too much.

311   to **bore**

Mel and Chip are **both** cute.

Both today and tomorrow

315   both

316   bottle

317   bottle opener

318   bottom

A **boulder** is a large piece of rock.

319   boulder

It **bounces** on the ground.

320   to **bounce**

A **bouquet** of flowers

321   bouquet

Bow and arrow

322   bow

324   bowl

What is inside the **box**?

325   box

326   boxer

323   bow tie

327   boy

328   bra

329   bracelet

Carla **brags** about her new toys.

Her dad tells her not to **brag**.

330   to **brag**

We use our **brains** to think.

331   brain

Every car has **brakes**.

332   brake

333   to **brake**

The **branch** of a big tree

334   branch

The dentist said you were very **brave**.

335   brave

336   bread

337   to **break**

338   to **break down**

A robber **broke in.**

339   to **break in**

We eat **breakfast** in the morning.

340   **breakfast**

Dragons have hot **breath.**

341   **breath**

342   to **breathe**

Is your house made of **bricks?**

343   **brick**

Pam is building a **brick** wall.

344   **bricklayer**

The **bride** is shy.

345   **bride**

So is the **bridegroom.**

346   **bridegroom**

347   **bridge**

A **bridle** for the horse

348   **bridle**

349   **briefcase**

350   **bright** sun

Torp **brings** my slippers.

351   to **bring**

Ashley **brings** back her library books.

352   to **bring back**

353   **brittle** glass

354   **broccoli**

355   **brooch**

A **brook** is a small river.

356   **brook**

357   **broom**

358   I love my **brother.**

359   brow

360   brown

Sean needs to **brush** his hair.

362   to brush

363   brush

That is a bad **bruise.**

361   bruise

366   brussels sprouts

364   paintbrush

365   toothbrush

367   bubble

368   bucket

369   belt buckle

370   bud

371   buffalo

372   bug

The soldier plays the **bugle.**

373   bugle

374   to build

375   bull

376   bulldozer

Bullets are dangerous.

377   bullet

378 bullhorn/megaphone*

Charlie is a big **bully**.

379   bully

380   bump

381   bumpers

A **bunch** of asparagus

382   bunch

383   bundle

384   buoy

385   burglar

The fire **burns** brightly.

386   to burn

His balloon **burst**.

387   to burst

388   to bury

389   bus

390   bus stop

A **bush** is smaller than a tree.

391   bush

392   I am **busy** now.

I would like to go, **but** I am busy.

Paul is big, **but** his sister is bigger.

But for you, we would have lost the game.

393   but

394   butcher

Some **butter** for my bread

395   butter

396   butterfly

397   buttons

Phil **buys** an ice cream.

398   to buy

399   cabbage

A **cabin** in the forest

400   cabin

401   cabinet

402   cable/lead*

403   cactus

404   cage

405   cake

406   calculator

407   calendar

408   calf

409   to **call**

Ashley is always **calm**.

412   She is **calm**.

413   camel

414   camera

We will **call off** the picnic if it rains.

Ashley has **called off** our trip to the zoo.

410   to **call off**

They are **camping** together.

415   to camp

416   campsite

417   can

411 to **call up**/to **phone***

418 can opener/tin* opener

Ships travel through the **canal**.

419   canal

420   canary

421   candle

422   candlestick

423   candy/sweets*

Grandpa uses a **walking stick**.

424   cane/walking stick*

425   cannon

426   I cannot see.

427   canoe

Cantaloupe is a type of melon.

428   cantaloupe

The river is in the **canyon**.

429   canyon

430   cap

A **cape** is the narrow tip of a continent.

431   cape

432   cape

M is a **capital** letter.

Paris is the **capital** of France.

The money you have saved up is your **capital**.

433   capital

He is the **captain** of his ship.

434   captain

435   to capture

436   car

A **caravan** crosses the desert.

437   caravan

438   cards

This box is made of **cardboard.**
439   cardboard

The nurse **cares** for the sick.
440   to **care**

Careless today, sorry tomorrow.
441   He is **careless.**

442   cargo

443   carnation

A **carnival** is one big party.
444   carnival

445   carpenter

446   carpet

447   carriage/pram*

448   carrot

Mr. Brown always **carries** too much.
449   to **carry**

450   cart

A **carton** of screws
451   carton

452   to carve

453   case

Cash is money.
454   cash

455   cashew nuts

456   castle

457   cat

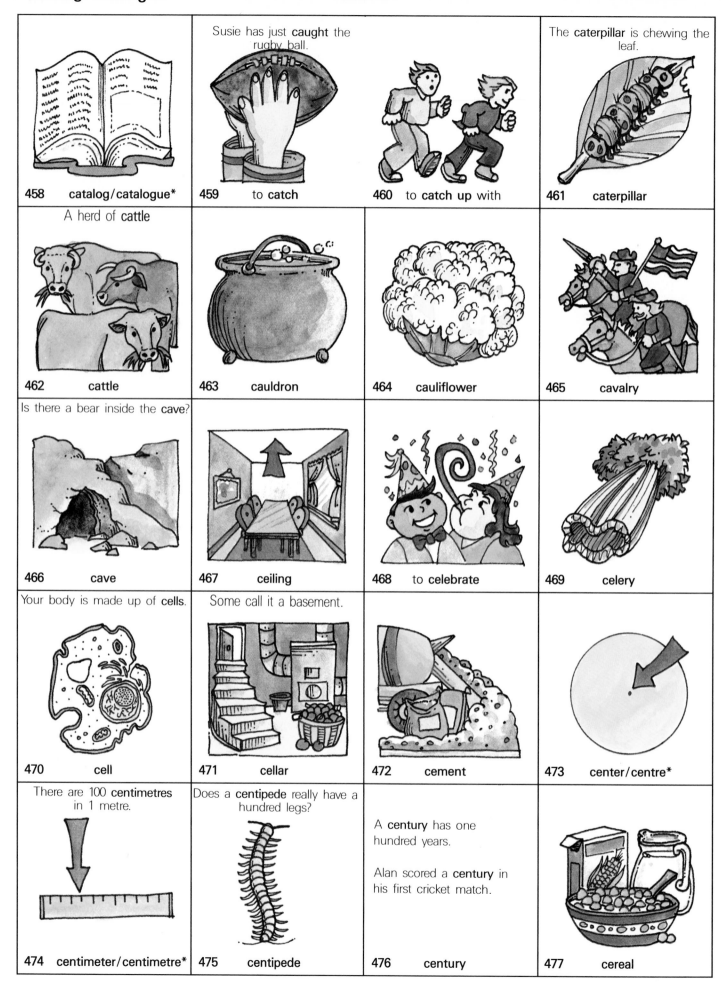

458   catalog/catalogue*

Susie has just **caught** the rugby ball.

459   to **catch**

460   to **catch up** with

The **caterpillar** is chewing the leaf.

461   caterpillar

A herd of **cattle**

462   cattle

463   cauldron

464   cauliflower

465   cavalry

Is there a bear inside the **cave**?

466   cave

467   ceiling

468   to **celebrate**

469   celery

Your body is made up of **cells**.

470   cell

Some call it a basement.

471   cellar

472   cement

473   center/centre*

There are 100 **centimetres** in 1 metre.

474   centimeter/centimetre*

Does a **centipede** really have a hundred legs?

475   centipede

A **century** has one hundred years.

Alan scored a **century** in his first cricket match.

476   century

477   cereal

478   certain

Ashley is **certain** that she is right.

She has a **certain** feeling about Tim, but she can't quite explain why.

479   certificate

480   chain

481   chainsaw

482   chair

483   chalk

484   champion

485   change

This is the **change** I got from a £5 note.

487   channel

488   chapter

This book has many **chapters**.

489   character

Ashley has a strong **character**.

She is quite a **character**.

What does this **character** mean?

486   to change

Carl **changed** his clothes.

490   charcoal

491   chard

Chard is a kind of vegetable.

492   to charge

The police **charged** Spud with robbery.

Your toy has stopped because I forgot to **charge** the battery.

They **charged** me a lot of money for this coat.

493   chariot

494   chart

495   to chase

496   to chat

497   cheap pencil, expensive crown

Gary is trying to **cheat** by looking at Mary's answers.

498 to **cheat**

Did you **check** your watch this morning?

499 to **check**

500 **cheek**

Cheese is made from milk.

501 **cheese**

Cheques are used to pay for things.

502 **cheque***/check

503 **cherries**

His waistcoat barely covers his **chest**.

504 **chest**

505 **chestnut**

Chew well before you swallow.

506 to **chew**

507 **chick peas**

508 **chicken**

509 **chicken-pox**

The **chief** is saluting.

510 **chief**

511 **child**

512 a **chilly** day

513 **chimney**

514 **chimpanzee**

515 **chin**

516 **china**/crockery*

A **chip** never falls far from the tree.

517 **chip**

The sculptor uses a **chisel**.
518 chisel

Chives taste like onions.
519 chives

A **chocolate** bar
520 chocolate

Do you sing in a **choir**?
521 choir

Choking someone is not a joke.
522 to **choke**

Peter **choked** on the bone.
523 to **choke on**

Which one should I **choose**?
524 to **choose**

Chopping onions
525 to **chop**

526 chopsticks

Chrome is a type of metal.
527 chrome

528 chrysanthemum

529 a **chunk/lump*** of coal

This **cigar** stinks!
530 cigar

Cigarettes make you sick.
531 cigarette

532 circle

533 circus

Do you live in a big **city**?
534 city

A **clam** lives in its shell.
535 clam

Held together with a **clamp**
536 clamp

537 to **clap**

538 classroom

The crab has strong **claws.**

539 claw

Clay is used to make bricks.

You can also make pots and dishes out of **clay.**

540 clay

541 She is all **clean.**

Aunt Betty **clears** the table.

542 to clear

543 cliff

Climbing to the top

544 to climb

545 clinic

546 to clip

547 clock

548 to close

Do you keep your **cupboard** neat?

549 closet/cupboard*

Clothes are made out of **cloth.**

There is a table**cloth** on the table.

I need a fresh drying-up **cloth** for all these dishes.

550 cloth

551 clothes

552 clothes line

553 cloud

A four-leaf **clover** is lucky.

554 clover

555 clown

Thal uses his **club** to hunt.

556 club

The police found a **clue** to the crime.

Sheila does not have a **clue** how to get there.

I will give you a **clue.**

557 clue

The **clutch** pedal is on the left.	**Clutch** the rope tightly!	Meet my **coach**.	We are travelling by **coach**.
558 clutch	559 to **clutch**	560 coach	561 coach
Coal comes from a mine.	This cloth is very **coarse**. Do not use **coarse** language!		Priscilla **coaches** the team twice a week.
563 coal	564 coarse	565 coast	562 to **coach**
You need a warm **coat** in winter.	A **cobweb** is the spider's home.		
566 coat	567 cobweb	568 cocoa	569 coconut
	Coffee beans grow on trees.		
570 cod	571 coffee	572 coffin	573 coil
			Ashley's sister **collects** stamps.
574 coin	575 I am **cold**.	576 collar	577 to **collect**

College is a school for bigger children and adults.

578   college

579   to **collide**

A bad **collision**

580   collision

Which is your favourite **colour**?

581   color/colours*

A mare and her **colt**

582   colt

Stone **columns**

583   column

584   comb

585   to **comb**

Combine them together.

586   combine

Tell Gordon to **come** home.

Ashley **came** to the party by bus.

Do you **come** here often?

Come on, tell me!

587   to **come**

It **came off** in my hand.

588   to **come off**

He fainted, but quickly **came to**.

589   to **come to**

590   comfortable

A real **comma** is smaller than this.

591   comma

592   to **command**

We live in a small **community**.

There is a pool at the **community** centre.

Building the centre was a **community** effort.

593   community

Tom is Tim's **companion**.

594   companion

595   I am in good **company**.

596   to **compare**

All **compasses** point North!

597   My **compass** points north.

Ludwig **composes** a symphony.

A **composition** on the piano

598 to **compose**	599 **composer**	600 **composition**	601 **computer**
602 to **concentrate**	603 **concert**	604 **concrete**	605 **conductor**
607 **cone**	608 ice cream **cone**	609 pine **cone**	606 **conductor/guard***

I am not sure which is the right way.

610 **confident**	611 I am **confused**	612 to **congratulate**	613 to **connect**

B, c, d, f, g
are the first five **consonants**
in the alphabet.

A police **constable** can help you.

A **constellation** is a group of many stars.

There are seven **continents** on Earth.

614 **consonant**	615 **constable**	616 **constellation**	617 **continent**

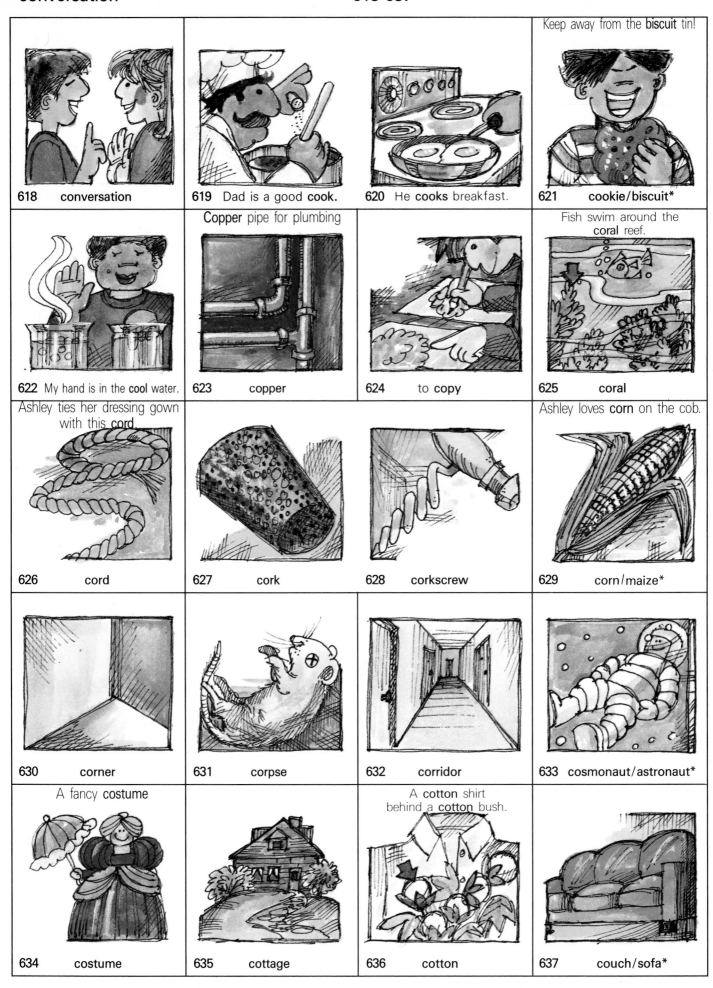

618 conversation

619 Dad is a good **cook.**

620 He **cooks** breakfast.

Keep away from the **biscuit** tin!
621 cookie/biscuit*

622 My hand is in the **cool** water.

Copper pipe for plumbing
623 copper

624 to **copy**

Fish swim around the **coral** reef.
625 coral

Ashley ties her dressing gown with this **cord.**
626 cord

627 cork

628 corkscrew

Ashley loves **corn** on the cob.
629 corn/maize*

630 corner

631 corpse

632 corridor

633 cosmonaut/astronaut*

A fancy **costume**
634 costume

635 cottage

A **cotton** shirt behind a **cotton** bush.
636 cotton

637 couch/sofa*

Kim **coughs** politely.			Put it on the **counter**!
638 to cough	**639** to count	**640** counter	**641** counter
Have you been to the **country**?	This **country** is Canada.	Mum and Dad are a **couple**.	It takes **courage** to fight dragons.
642 country	**643** country	**644** couple	**645** courage
A tennis **court**			Keep the **cover** on the jar.
646 court	**647** My **cousin** is my uncle's daughter.	**648** to cover	**649** cover
			Crabs live in the sea.
650 cow	**651** This boy is a **coward**.	**652** cowboy	**653** crab
This jar has a **crack** in it.			
654 crack	**655** cracker	**656** cradle	**657** crane

658   crane

659   to **crash**

What is inside the **crate**?

660   crate

661   to **crawl**

662   crayfish

663   crayons

Dad likes **cream** in his coffee.

Ice **cream** is very sweet.

Sun **cream** protects your skin.

664   cream

665   crease

What a strange **creature**!

666   creature

A **creek** is a small river.

667   creek

668   the **crew**

669   crib/cot*

670   cricket

671   criminal

672   crocodile

Crocuses are a sign of spring.

673   crocus

That **crook** stole an apple!

674   crook

675   crooked post

The leaning picture of Pisa

676 **crooked** painting, upright tower

This farmer has grown a healthy **crop** of maize.

677   crop

Look before you **cross**!

678   cross

679   to **cross**

680   to **cross out**

681   crow

682   A big **crowd** in a small space.

683   **crown**

Sir Peter **crowns** the new Queen.

684   to **crown**

685   **crumb**

Crushing grapes for wine

686   to **crush**

Ashley likes the **crust** best.

687   **crust**

688   crutch

689   to cry

A **crystal** ball

690   crystal

A **cub** is a baby bear.

691   cub

692   cube

693   cuckoo

694   cucumber

695   cuff

A **cup** of tea

696   cup

The jar is in the **cupboard**.

697   cupboard

		Samantha **curls** her hair.	Now she has **curly** hair.
698 curb/kerb*	699 I am **cured**.	700 to **curl**	701 **curly**

		A strong **current**	
702 curious	703 currant	704 current	705 curtains

| 706   curve | 707   cushion | 708   customer | 709   to cut |

| 712   cute/sweet* | 713   cutlery | 714   cycle | 710   to **cut in** |

			Cut out the paper doll !
715 cylinder	716 cymbals	717 cypress	711 to **cut out**

A **daffodil** is a spring flower.

Fido collects the **daily** newspaper.

718	daffodil	719	dagger	720	daily

Cows live on a **dairy** farm.

A **dam** across the river

| 721 | dairy | 722 | daisy | 723 | dam | 724 | damaged |

Dandelions are weeds.

| 725 | damp | 726 | to dance | 727 | dancer | 728 | dandelion |

Not afraid of the **dark**

Darts are for throwing.

| 729 | danger | 730 | dark | 731 | dart | 732 | dashboard |

What is the **date** today?

This is my **daughter** Penelope.

| 733 | date | 734 | daughter | 735 | the start of a nice **day** | 736 | **dead** mouse |

The **deaf** cannot hear.

737   deaf

Chuck is my **dear** friend.

Dear Mum, this trip is fun!

Oh **dear**, I forgot my purse.

738   dear

December is the last month of the year.

739   December

Ashley cannot **decide** what to wear.

Mum may have to **decide** for her.

740   to decide

The **deck** of a ship

741   deck

Phil the pirate **decorates** the tree.

742   to decorate

743   decoration

Albert avoids the **deep** end.

744   deep end

There are **deer** in the woods.

745   deer

746   to deliver

Tom **dented** my car.

747   to dent

748   dentist

749   department store

750   desert

Who put this **desk** in the desert?

751   desk

752   dessert

Godzilla **destroys** the city.

753   to destroy

A kind of warship

754   destroyer

755   detective

Morning **dew** on the leaves

756   dew

757 diagonal	**758** diagram	Diamonds are precious stones which sparkle. **759** diamond	Babies need **nappies**. **760** diaper/nappy*
Do you keep a **diary**? **761** diary	Look it up in the **dictionary**. **762** dictionary	**763** to die	All people are born equal, there is no **difference** between them. There is quite a **difference** between night and day. **764** difference
...but all equal **765** different people	**766** to dig	Good luck, snake! **767** The snake **digests** an elephant.	A very **dim** room **768** dim
Ashley has **dimples** in her cheeks. **769** dimple	**770** dinghy	**771** dining room	**772** dinner
773 dinosaur	This way! **774** direction	Daddy stepped into the **dirt**. **775** dirt	His trousers are really **dirty**. **776** dirty

I **disagree** with you, we have different opinions.

777   to **disagree**

The apple has **disappeared**.

778   to **disappear**

779   **disaster**

780   to **discover**

781   to **discuss**

782   **disease**

Ashley wears a **disguise**.

783   **disguise**

Please wash the **dishes**! Ashley, where are you?

784   **dishes**

785   a **dishonest** person

786   **dishwater**

787   to **dislike**

The tablet **dissolves** in water.

788   to **dissolve**

789   **distance** between two trees

A **distant** tree is far away.

790   a **distant** tree

The **district** where I live

791   **district**

We are digging a **ditch** to drain the field.

792   **ditch**

793   to **dive**

To **divide** an apple

794   to **divide**

795   I feel **dizzy**.

I have to **do** something to fix the stool.

796   What shall I **do**?

| 797 dock | 798 doctor | 799 dog | 800 doll |

| 801 dolphin | 802 dome | The **donkey** carries a heavy load.
803 donkey | 804 door |

| 805 doorknob | 806 double | 807 dough | The **dove** is a symbol of peace.
808 dove |

| Ashley has a **down** pillow.
809 down | 810 to doze | Twelve eggs to a **dozen**
811 dozen | Do not **drag** it in the dirt!
812 to drag |

| 813 dragon | 814 dragonfly | 815 drain/plug hole* | Roy **draws** very well.
816 to draw |

Raise the **drawbridge**!

817   drawbridge

Ashley's socks are not in this **drawer**.

818   drawer

819   a nice **dream**

Ron **dreams** even when he is not sleeping.

820   I **dream** of sheep.

821   dress

822   to dress

Maybe Ashley's socks are in this **chest of drawers**.

823   dresser/chest of drawers*

824   to dribble

It is no fun to **drift** on the ocean.

825   to drift

Pam **drills** tiny holes.

826   to drill

827   drill

828   drink

The tap is **dripping**.

830   to drip

831   I **drive** carefully.

832   crazy **driver**

829   to drink

The rain has become a light **drizzle**.

833   drizzle

834   to drool

One **drop** at a time

835   drop

Our guest **dropped** the glass.

836   to drop

Drop in to see me anytime.

837　　　to drop in

838　Dad drops off the cat at the vet.

He dropped out of the race.

839　　　to drop out

I am almost asleep.

840　　I feel drowsy.

841　　　drum

842　　　dry

843　　　to dry

844　　　dry cleaner

Put the wet laundry in the dryer.

845　　　dryer

The duchess is married to the duke.

846　　　duchess

847　　　duck

A duel is not a good way to settle an argument.

848　　　duel

849　　　duke

A rubbish dump

850　　　dump

851　　　to dump

852　　dumptruck/lorry*

The thief has been locked in the dungeon a long time.

853　　　dungeon

854　　　dusk

855　　　dust

856　　　dwarf

E

857 Each rabbit has a carrot.

858 eagle

859 ear

860 early

Mum **earns** a good wage.

Ashley has **earned** a holiday.

You must **earn** it before you spend it.

861 to earn

The planet **Earth**

862 Earth

Shovelling **earth**

863 earth

864 earthquake

865 easel

East and west are opposites.

866 east

867 Swimming is **easy.**

868 to eat

869 to eat breakfast

870 to eat lunch

871 to eat dinner/supper*

Hello..ello...lo...

872 echo

A solar **eclipse**

873 eclipse

874 The tree is at the **edge.**

875 eel

The hen laid an **egg**.

876   egg

877   eggplant/aubergine*

878   eight

879   eighth

Reg streches the **elastic**.

880   elastic

881   elbow

Elections are held to choose the government.

Who won the **election**?

The **election** was very close.

882   election

883   electrician

884   electricity

885   elephant

886   elevator/lift*

887   elk

888   elm

Stephen has **embarrassed** him.

889   to embarrass

890   to embrace

891   embroidery

892   emergency

893   The jar is **empty**.

The **end** of the road

894   This is the **end**.

Some day they will stop being **enemies**.

895   enemies

The **engine** of a car makes it go.

896   engine

897 engineer/engine driver*

898   to **enjoy**

899   **enormous** dinosaur

900   That is **enough**.

901   to **enter**

902   entrance

903   envelope

904   equal

The **equator** divides the Earth into two hemispheres.

905   equator

Ashley is running an **errand** for Dad.

906   errand

One **escalator** moves up and one moves down.

907   escalator

He barely **escaped**.

908   to **escape**

Europe is a continent.

909   Europe

910   evaporation

911   Four is an **even** number.

912   an **even** surface

913   evergreen

Ashley makes her bed almost **every** day.

Must Mum tell her **every** time?

914   every

Some **exams** are easy.

915   exam

916 to examine	Sometimes Ashley does not set a good **example**. Things are easier to understand when you give an **example**. **917** example	**918** exclamation mark	**919** Excuse me!
Karen **exercises** to stay healthy. **920** to exercise	To **exist** is to be. Ashley said "There is no such thing", and she meant "It does not **exist**". **921** to exist	**922** to exit/leave*	The balloon will **expand** until it bursts. **923** to expand
We **expect** you at two o'clock. Dad **expects** you to be good. Anne cannot **expect** any more. **924** to expect	An **expensive** watch costs a lot of money. **925** expensive	**926** experiment	Marjorie is an **expert** on books. **927** expert
Let me **explain** it to you. **928** to explain	Charlie is **exploring** in the jungle. **929** to explore	**930** explosion	A fire **extinguisher** **931** extinguisher

932   eye

933   eyebrow

934 eyeglasses/spectacles*

935   eyelash

F

Pam read a **fable** about the ant and the grasshopper.

936   **fable**

937   **face**

938   **factory**

Tom has **failed** his exams.

939   to **fail**

940   to **fail**

941   **fair**

The **fairy** will grant you a wish.

942   **fairy**

We have **faith** in you.

Ashley accepted it in good **faith**.

943   **faith**

This one is a **fake**, it is not genuine.

944   **fake** painting

The leaves fall in the **autumn**.

945   **fall/autumn***

946   to **fall**

They thought the house was on fire.

949   **false** alarm

These people are related to each other.

950   **family**

947   to **fall down**

948   to **fall off**

Marilyn is a **famous** star.

951   **famous** actress

952   **fan**

953   **fancy** clothes

954   **fang**

955   The city is **far** away.

956   **Farewell**!

Our food comes from the **farm**.

957   **farm**

958   **farmer**

959   **fast**

Never forget to **fasten** it!

960   I **fasten** my seatbelt.

Hector likes sugar.

961   **fat**

Drinking poison is **fatal**.

962   **fatal**

963   **father**

The **tap** is dripping.

964   **faucet/tap***

They both say it is the other's **fault**.

965   Whose **fault** is it?

Can you do me a **favour**?

Ashley is kind and likes doing people **favours**.

966   **favor/favour***

My **favourite** flavour

967   **favorite/favourite***

968   to **fear** the worst

969   **feast**

A bird must have lost this **feather**.

970   **feather**

The second month of the year

971   **February**

Elaine **feeds** the baby.

972   to **feed**

973   I **feel** well.

The **female** bird lays the eggs.

974   **female**

975   fence

976   fender/wing*

977   fern

978   ferry

979   festival

Paul has a bad **fever**.
980   fever

981   **Few** people came.

982   field

Alice is **fifth**.
983   fifth

They are bad and **fight** a lot.
984   to fight

985   to file

986   to fill

A **film** for her camera
988   film

One **filthy** pig
989   filthy

That **fin** belongs to a shark.
990   fin

987   to fill up

A **fine** for speeding
991   fine

992   I am **fine**.

993   finger

994   fingerprint

Ashley's friend **finished** first.

995 to finish

Fir trees have needles.

996 fir

997 fire

998 fire engine

999 fire escape

Beware! **Fireworks** can be dangerous!

1000 firecracker/banger*

1001 firefighter

1002 fireplace

Ashley has a **firm** handshake.

Penny's **firm** makes toys.

Dad's decision is **firm**, Tom cannot have another ice cream.

1003 firm

First in line

1004 first

1005 fish

1006 to fish

1007 fishhook

1008 fist

1009 five

Do you think he can **fix** it?

1010 to fix

A pirate **flag**

1011 flag

1012 flake

1013 flame

Tweeter is **flapping** his wings.

1014 to flap

A **flare** can light up the night.			
1015 flare	1016 flash	1017 flashlight/torch*	1018 flask
	To **flatten** dough	Which **flavour** do you like best?	Spot has a **flea** on his back.
1019 flat	1020 to flatten	1021 flavor/flavour*	1022 flea
Shelley **flees** for his life.		Quite a bit of **flesh**	
1023 to flee	1024 fleece	1025 flesh	1026 to float
A **flock** of birds			Jack needs **flour** for baking.
1027 flock	1028 flood	1029 floor	1030 flour
The blood **flows** into his vein.		Crispin is ill with the **flu**.	
1031 to flow	1032 flower	1033 flu	1034 fluff

Lemonade is a **fluid**.

1035   fluid

1036   fly

Do up your **fly**!

1037   fly

Birds and planes **fly**.

1038   to fly

1039   foam

You cannot see far in the **fog**.

1040   fog

Fold it this way.

1041   to fold

That goose **follows** Tom everywhere.

1042   to follow

1043   food

1044   foot

1045   American football

Footprint in the snow

1046   footprint

I hear **footsteps** behind me.

1047   footsteps

One **for** all and all **for** one.

For better or **for** worse

But **for** you, we would have lost the game.

1048   for

1049   to force

1050   forehead

There are animals in the **forest**.

1051   forest

Our dog **forgets** his name.

Dad **forgot** to buy milk.

Forget it!

1052   to forget

I **forgive** you if you promise to be good.

Ashley **forgave** her dog for eating her favourite doll.

1053   to forgive

1054   fork

1055   forklift

1056 form/tailor's dummy*

The soldiers are inside the **fort**.

1057   fort

Go **forward** until you reach the front door.

Ashley thinks he is too **forward**.

Are you looking **forward** to your birthday?

1058   forward

This **fossil** was once a fish.

1059   fossil

1060   foul odor/odour*

The **foundation** of a house

1061   foundation

1062   fountain

A sly **fox**

1063   fox

A **fraction** of the whole pie

1064   fraction

Eggs are very **fragile**.

1065   fragile

1066   frame

Do you have **freckles**, too?

1067   freckle

1068   free

Atuk's orange juice **froze**.

1069   to freeze

Picked **fresh** from the tree

1070   fresh

Friday is the last weekday.

1071   Friday

Fridge means refrigerator.

1072   fridge

1073   friends

Carla **frightens** him every time.

1074   to frighten

1075   frog

1076   I am **from** Mars.

1077   front

There is **frost** on the window.

1078   frost

What is he **frowning** about?

1079   to **frown**

Fruit is much better for you than chocolate.

1080   fruit

1081   to **fry**

1082   frying pan

1083   Cars need **fuel**.

1084   full

1085   having **fun**

This **fund** helps the poor.

1086   charity **fund**

They went to the **funeral**.

1087   funeral

Pour it through the **funnel**.

1088   funnel

Mother does not think that is **funny**.

A **funny** thing happened on the way to school.

Ashley felt **funny** after eating that mushroom.

1089   funny

A **fur** coat in the summer

1090   fur coat

The house would be cold without a **boiler**.

1092   furnace / boiler*

1093   furniture

A **fuse** is an electrical safety device.

1094   fuse

Fluffy is a **furry** cat.

1091   furry

A **gale** is a strong wind.

1095   gale

The art **gallery**

1096   gallery

A horse can canter, **gallop** or trot.

1097   to gallop

Shelby enjoys **games**.

1098   game

A **gander** is a male goose.

1099   gander

A **gang** of villains

1100   gang

Ashley has a **gap** between her front teeth.

1101   gap

The car is in the **garage**.

1102   garage

1103   garbage/rubbish*

1104   garbage can/rubbish bin*

1105   vegetable **garden**

1106   to gargle

Garlic has a strong taste.

1107   garlic

A **garter** keeps stockings up.

1108   garter

The balloon was filled with **gas**.

Some **gases** are lighter than air.

Firefighters wear **gas** masks to protect themselves.

1109   gas

1110   gas/petrol*

1111 gas pedal/accelerator*

1112 gas/petrol pump*

1113 gas/petrol station*

1114 gate	She is **gathering** flowers. **1115** to **gather**	**1116** gears	**1117** gem
A high-ranking officer **1118** general	**1119** a **generous** friend	**1120** a **gentle** person	Dad is a real **gentleman**. **1121** gentleman
1122 a **genuine** pig	We all study **geography**. **1123** geography	Geraniums are common pot plants. **1124** geranium	A pet **gerbil** **1125** gerbil
Germs cause disease. **1126** germ	Tigger the cat **gets** moving. **1127** **Get** that mouse!	**1128** I want to **get** it **back**.	Ashley **gets in** slowly. **1129** to **get in** the pool
Ashley **gets off**... **1130** to **get off**	then on... **1131** to **get on**	She **gets rid** of the rubbish... **1132** to **get rid of**	...but first she **gets up**. **1133** to **get up**

Are you afraid of **ghosts**?

1134   ghost

1135   giant

1136   gift

A **gigantic** whale

1137   gigantic

1138   to giggle

Fish breathe through **gills**.

1139   gills

Ginger is a spice.

1140   ginger

A tasty **gingerbread** man

1141   gingerbread

A **gipsy** caravan is always on the move.

1142   gipsy

Is a **giraffe** really higher than the sun?

1143   giraffe

1144   girl

She **gave** Anne the umbrella.

1145   to give

Glaciers are made of ice.

1148   glacier

1149   I am glad.

Windows are made of **glass**.

1150   glass

Anne **gave** it **back** when the rain stopped.

1146   to give back

Do you wear **glasses**?

1152   glasses

1153   to glide

A **glass** of water

1151   glass

1147   I give up!

A **glider** is a plane without an engine.

1154   glider

1155   gloves

Glue makes it stick.

1156   glue

1157   to **go**

The **goalkeeper** defends the **goal**.

1161   goal

A billy**goat** or a nanny**goat**?

1162   goat

The **goggles** protect her eyes.

1163   goggles

He **goes down** to work.

1158   to **go down**

A bar of **gold**

1164   gold

1165   goldfish

Uncle John plays **golf**.

1166   golf

Spot **goes in** for a nap.

1159   to **go in**

This food tastes **good.**

1167   good

1168   Goodbye!

1169   goose

Jack **goes up** the beanstalk.

1160   to **go up**

1170   gooseberry

She thinks she has a **gorgeous** hairdo.

1171   gorgeous

1172   gorilla

The government **governs** the country.

It is not as easy to **govern** a country as it seems.

There are rules **governing** how we play this game.

1173   to **govern**

The **government** is elected by the people.

Ashley's dad, the admiral, works for the **government.**

1174   government

He **grabbed** her ice cream and will be punished.

1175   to grab

1176   He is very **gracious.**

This is my school and I am in second **form.**

1177   grade / form*

We harvest **grain** to make flour.

1178   grain

1000 **grams** = 1 kilogram

1179   gram

1180   grandchild

1181   grandfather

Ashley's **grandmother** likes baking.

1182   grandmother

Granite is a hard rock.

1183   granite

I **grant** you ten days' leave of absence.

The good fairy will **grant** you three wishes.

1184   to grant

A bunch of **grapes**

1185   grapes

1186   grapefruit

1187   graph

1188   grass

1189   grasshopper

1190   grater

1191   grave

Loose **gravel** next to the road

1192   gravel

1193   **Gravity** makes apples fall.

Cows **graze** in the field.

1194   to **graze**

Grease will stop the squeaking.

1195   **grease**

1196   a **great** toy

1197   **greedy**

1198   **green**

1199   **green bean**

1200   **greenhouse**

Tom always **greets** a lady.

1201   to **greet**

1202   **grey*/gray**

1203   to **grill**

1204   **grimy**

Chuck **grins** because he is happy.

1205   to **grin**

Mum **minces** meat for dinner.

1206   to **grind**/to **mince***

Grip the handlebars tightly.

1207   to **grip**

1208   to **groan**

The **grocer** tells her where to look.

1209   **grocer**

The bride and **groom**

1211   **groom**

The **groom** takes care of the horse.

1212   **groom**

Pam is **grooming** herself.

1213   to **groom**

1210   shopping for **groceries**

1214 groove

This **gross** thing is overfed.

1215 gross/disgusting*

1216 ground

1217 groundhog

A **group** of people

1218 group

1219 to grow

1220 to growl

1221 grown-up

1222 to guard

Now, let me **guess**...

1223 to guess

His **guest** arrives to stay for the night.

1224 guest

He **guides** the guest to his room.

1225 to guide

Ashley says she did not do it - she is not **guilty**.

Who is **guilty** of this theft?

The thief who took the biscuit tin is certainly **guilty**.

1226 guilty

Guinea pigs eat a lot.

1227 guinea pig

1228 guitar

A **gulf** is part of the sea almost enclosed by land.

1229 Gulf of Mexico

Sea **gulls** live by the water.

1230 gull

Brush your **gums** to keep them healthy.

1231 gum

There are better habits than chewing **gum**.

1232 gum/chewing gum*

The water flows in the **gutter**.

1233 gutter

1234   bad **habit**

1235   **haddock**

A sudden **hail** storm

1236   **hail**

Ashley's sister has lots of **hair**.

1237   **hair**

1238   **hairbrush**

1239   **hairdresser**

This is not a small **hairdryer**.

1240   **hairdryer**

Do you want the other **half**?

1241   **half**

This space is a **hall**.

1242   **hall**

Halloween is trick or treat night.

1243   **Halloween/Hallowe'en***

This space is a **corridor**.

1244   **hallway/corridor***

The soldier **halted** outside the door.

1245   to **halt**

1246   **hammer**

Rob **hammered** in the nail.

1247   to **hammer**

1248   **hammock**

1249   **hamster**

1250   **hand**

1251   to **hand out**

Bicycles have **hand brakes**.

1252   **hand brake**

1253 handcuffs	Being blind is a **handicap**. People can overcome any **handicap**. 1254 handicap	1255 handle	1256 handrail
He thinks he is very **handsome**. 1257 handsome	1258 handy person	Hang the picture straight! 1259 to hang	1260 to hang on
Aeroplanes are kept in a **hangar**. 1262 hangar	Hang your coat on the **hanger**. 1263 hanger	1264 handkerchief	1261 to hang up
1265 Accidents **happen**.	1266 He is **happy**.	The ship docked in the **harbour**. 1267 harbor/harbour*	Too **hard** to break 1268 hard
1269 hare	Never **harm** an animal ! 1270 to harm	1271 harmonica	The horse is in a **harness**. 1272 harness

1273 harp	**1274** a **harsh** winter	Sam **harvests** the crop. **1275** to **harvest**	**1276** hat
The chick has **hatched.** **1277** to **hatch**	**1278** hatchet	Michael **hauls** a heavy load. **1279** to **haul**	**1280** **haunted** house
Pat **has** the doll Sharon wants. **1281** to **have**	**1282** hawk	**Hay** for the horses **1283** hay	**1284** **Haze** makes for a hazy day.
1285 hazel	**1286** hazelnut	**1287** head	**1288** I have a **headache.**
1289 headrest	His broken leg is **healing.** **1290** to **heal**	**1291** **healthy** flower	A big **pile** of rubbish **1292** heap/pile*

1293 I **hear** a voice.	1294 **heart**	1295 to **heat**	1296 **heater/radiator***
1297 to **heave**	1298 **heaven**	1299 one **heavy** elephant	A neat **hedge** round the garden is very nice. 1300 **hedge**
A **hedgehog** is not a porcupine. 1301 **hedgehog**	1302 **heel**	1303 **helicopter**	1304 **hell**
1305 **hello**	At the **helm** of the ship 1306 **helm**	Soldiers wear **helmets.** 1307 **helmet**	Gail's mum **helps** to start the car. 1308 to **help**
A small baby is **helpless.** 1309 **helpless**	1310 **hem**	The equator divides the Earth into two **hemispheres.** 1311 **hemisphere**	1312 **hen**

A **heptagon** has seven sides.

1313   heptagon

1314   herbs

A **herd** of cattle

1315   herd

1316   Come **here**!

A **hermit** lives alone.

1317   hermit

1318   hero

1319   heroine

1320   herring

Paul **hesitates** before diving in.

1321   to **hesitate**

A **hexagon** has six sides.

1322   hexagon

Bears **hibernate** all winter.

1323   to **hibernate**

1324   to **hiccup/hiccough***

The **hide** of an animal is its skin.

1325   hide

1326   to **hide**

1327   hiding-place

1328   a **high** mountain

1329   highrise/tower block*

1330   high school/secondary school*

1331   highway/motorway***

1332   to **hijack** a plane

There is a tree at the top of the **hill**.

1333   hill

1334   hinge

1335   hind legs

1336   hand on **hip**

Some call it a hippo.

1337   hippopotamus

1338   I study **history**.

Hit it straight on the head.

1339   to **hit**

Bees live in a bee**hive**.

1340   hive

1341   to **hoard**

1342   **hoarse** voice

Mum's **hobby** is knitting.

1343   hobby

My brother plays ice **hockey**.

1344   hockey/ice hockey*

1347   hoe

Ashley is **holding** Tigger the cat.

1348   to **hold**

Ashley should not **hold** him **down** like that.

1349   to **hold down**

1345   hockey puck

1350   hole

Uncle Jack has worked hard for this **holiday**.

1351   holiday

Squirrels live in **hollow** trees.

1352   **hollow** tree

1346   hockey stick

Holly and its berries

1353 holly

In certain places cows are **holy**.

1354 a **holy** cow

The squirrels are at **home**.

1355 home

1356 homework

Fred says he loves me.

1357 Is he **honest**?

Bears love **honey**.

1358 honey

1359 honeycomb

1360 honeydew melon

1361 to **honk**

1362 honor/honour*

Ashley's coat has a **hood**.

1363 hood

The engine is under the **bonnet**.

1364 hood/bonnet*

Horses have **hooves**.

1365 hoof

1366 hook

1367 jump through a **hoop**

1368 to **hop**

George **hopes** to be first.

1369 I **hope** to win.

One **hopeless** rider

1370 hopeless

1371 hopscotch/hop-scotch*

The sun rises over the **horizon**.

1372 horizon

1373 horizontal

1374 horn

1375 French horn

1376 horn

A **hornet** can sting.

1377 hornet

1378 horse

Horseradish tastes hot!

1379 horseradish

A lucky **horseshoe**

1380 horseshoe

1381 hose

1382 hospital

It is really **hot.**

1383 hot

So **hot**, my tongue is burning.

1384 hot

We stay in **hotels** when we travel.

1386 hotel

One **hour** has sixty minutes.

1387 hour

1388 hourglass

How hot do you think it is?

1385 hot pepper

1389 house

A **hovercraft** travels over water and land.

1390 hovercraft

1391 I will show you **how.**

The wolf **howls** at the moon.

1392 to howl

1393   hub cap

1394   huckleberry

1395   to huddle

1396   huge

1397   hull

1398   hummingbird

1399   hump

1400   hundred

Who names the **hurricanes**?

1401   She is **hungry.**

1402   to hunt

1403   to hurl

1404   hurricane

1405   to hurry

1406   My wrist **hurts.**

Husband and wife

1407   husband

1408   hut

1409   hutch/sideboard*

1410   hyacinth

The choir sings a **hymn.**

1411   hymn

Hyphens are short lines between words that belong together.

1412   hyphen

Ice cubes in a glass

1413 ice

1414 ice cream

Icebergs can sink ships.

1415 iceberg

1416 icicle

Icing on the cake

1417 icing

I think she just had an idea!

1418 idea

Can you tell us apart?

1419 identical twins

1420 idiot

1421 idle

If I had a hammer, I would only hammer when no one was sleeping.

I would buy it for you if I could.

1422 if

1423 igloo

1424 ignition key

Paul has been ill for days.

1425 ill

1426 to illuminate

Pictures in a book are called illustrations.

This dictionary has many illustrations.

1427 illustration

This is an important matter.

What is important to Ashley may not be important to Jack.

1428 important

Is Tony in?

Go and jump in the lake!

In time, we will find out who took the biscuit tin.

1429 in

An incense burner

1430 incense

Twelve inches make a foot.

1431 inch

There is an **index** at the back of the book.

The **index** contains all the words in this dictionary.

1432   index

1433   indigo

Carla has decided to stay **indoors**.

1434   indoors

1435   infant

Aunt Sylvia has an **infection**.

1436   infection

Her condition is **infectious**.

You could catch an **infectious** disease.

Dad has an **infectious** laugh.

1437   infectious

It is not nice to **inform** on someone.

1438   to inform

1439   The bear **inhabits** a cave.

What are your **initials**?

1440   initials

An **injection** in the arm

1441   injection

1442   injury

Ink is used for writing.

1443   ink

There are many different **insects**.

1444   insect

Inside the box

1445   inside

I **insist** that you have a bath.

1446   to insist

Fred **inspects** the leaf for disease.

1447   to inspect

A spoon for the soup

1449   Use a spoon **instead** of a fork!

Follow **instructions** to do the job properly.

1450   instruction

1451   instructor

1448   inspector

There is **insulation** in the walls of the house.

There is **insulation** around the wires so people will not get a shock.

1452 insulation

1453 intersection/crossroads*

She asked him why he wanted the job.

1454 interview

Daniel goes **into** the room.

1455 into the room

Marg **introduces** them to each other.

1456 to introduce

Vikings **invaded** other countries.

1457 to invade

Some became **invalids**.

1458 invalid

Did he really **invent** trees?

1459 to invent

The **invisible** man

1460 invisible

You are **invited** to our party.

1461 invitation

Please come!

1462 He is **inviting** her.

1463 iris

Mel **irons** all his clothes.

1464 to iron

1465 iron

1466 iron mask

You can reach the **island** by boat.

1467 island

Ashley got a bad **itch** from the stinging nettles.

The **itch** will go away if she does not scratch.

1468 itch

1469 to itch

1470 My skin is **itchy**.

Ivy grows on walls.

1471 ivy

Luke **jabbed** me in the side.

1472   to **jab**

Is this **jacket** the right size?

1473   **jacket**

Some books have dust **jackets**.

1474   dust **jacket**

Be careful not to cut yourself!

1475   **jagged** edge

1476   **jail/gaol***

1477   **jam**

Martin **jammed** his foot in the door.

1478   to **jam**

The first month of the year

1479   **January**

1480   **jar**

This shark has **JAWS.**

1481   **jaw**

1482   **jeans**

1483   **jeep**

Jelly for dessert

1484   **jelly**

1485   **jet** engine

1486   **jet** plane

A precious **jewel**

1488   **jewel**

1489   **jigsaw puzzle**

1490   doing a **job**

1487   **jet** of water

The **jockey** rides a racehorse.

1491   jockey

1492   to jog

Join the ends together.

1493   to join

The elbow **joint**

1494   joint

Uncle Burt thinks this is a good **joke**.

1495   joke

The **judge** will decide.

1496   judge

1497   juggler

Fresh orange **juice**

1498   juice

July is the seventh month of the year.

1499   July

1500   to jump

1501   to jump in

1502   to jump on

Mel is a good **jumper**.

1503   jumper

1504   jumper/pinafore*

These are useful to start a car.

1505   jumper cables/jump leads*

June is a good time for tennis.

1506   June

There are tigers in the **jungle**.

1507   jungle

A **junk** is a Chinese boat.

1508   junk

Junk also means rubbish.

1509   junk

Ashley **just** got home.

Just a little, thanks.

The judge is a **just** person.

1510   just

K

A **kaleidoscope** produces many beautiful patterns.
1511   kaleidoscope

1512   kangaroo

The **keel** of a boat keeps it steady.
1513   keel

Spot likes his **kennel**.
1514   kennel

1515   kernel

1516   kettle

1517   key

1518   to kick

This **kid** is my friend.
1519   kid

Goats have **kids** too.
1520   kid

Only criminals **kidnap** people.
1521   to kidnap

1522   kidney

A hunter **killed** the lion.
1523   to kill

Clay pots bake in a **kiln**.
1524   kiln

1 **kilogram** = 1000 grams
1525   kilogram

1 **kilometre** = 1000 metres
1526   kilometer/kilometre*

Men wear **kilts** in Scotland.
1527   kilt

A dress is a **kind** of garment. 1528

1529   kind girl

1530 king	1531 kingfisher	A newspaper **kiosk** 1532 kiosk	**Kippers** are a type of smoked herring. 1533 kippers
1534 to kiss	Give me a **kiss**. 1535 kiss	1536 kitchen	Flying a **kite** 1537 kite
The **kitten** will grow into a cat. 1538 kitten	1539 kiwi	1540 knee	1541 to kneel
1542 knife	Can you **knit** a sweater? 1543 to knit	A door **knob** 1544 knob	**Knock** on the door. 1545 to knock
1546 knot	Do you **know** what it means? Ashley **knows** some French. 1547 to know	1548 knuckle	**Koalas** live in Australia. 1549 koala bear

L

1550   **label**
There is a warning on the **label**.

1551   **laboratory**

1552   **lace**
A fine **lace** collar

1554   **ladder**

1555   **ladle**

1556   **lady**

1553   to **lace**
Bob **laces** up his shoes.

1557   **ladybug/ladybird***

1558   **ladyfingers**
Ladyfingers are cakes in America and vegetables in Britain.

1559   **lair**
The monster is in his **lair**.

1560   **lake**
Lakes are surrounded by land.

1561   **lamb**
A **lamb** is a baby sheep.

1562   **lame**
Flossie has a **lame** leg.

1563   **lamp**

1564   **lamp-post**

1565   **lance**

1566   **land**

1567   to **land**

1568   **landing**

The flat we live in belongs to our **landlord**.

We pay our **landlord** rent every month.

1569 landlord

Some motorways have many **lanes**.

1570 lane

How many **languages** can you speak?

English is Ashley's first **language**.

Ashley wants to learn another **language**.

1571 language

1572 lantern

The baby is sitting on her **lap**.

1573 lap

1574 larch

Lard is used for cooking.

1575 lard

1576 large

1577 lark

An eye**lash**

1578 lash

1579 the last piece

1580 Some things do last.

Latch the door, please.

1581 to latch

People are upset when you are **late**.

1582 You are late.

Lather for shaving

1583 lather

1584 to laugh

The **launch** took Mr. and Mrs. Walker ashore.

1585 launch

1586 to launch

1587 launchpad

1588 laundry/washing*

1589   laundry/launderette*

1590   lavender

The **law** is the same for everybody.
1591   Obey the **law**!

Did you mow the **lawn**?
1592   lawn

1594   to **lay** tiles

1595   **layer** upon **layer**

1596   He is **lazy**.

1593   lawn mower

Vincent **leads** the horse.
1597   to **lead**

The **leader** of the group
1598   leader

1599   leaf

This bucket **leaks**.
1600   to **leak**

The **leaning** tower of Pisa
1601   to **lean**

1602   I **learn** to read.

1603   leash/lead*

1604   Shoes are made of **leather**.

I will just **leave** it here.
1605   to **leave**

Tony is **leaving**.
1606   to **leave**

1607   **ledge** of a window

1608   leek

Turn **left** at the corner.

1609   left

1610   He is **left-handed.**

A pair of **legs**

1611   leg

The **legend** of the Cyclops

1612   legend

1613   lemon

1614   lemonade

I will **lend** you this book.

1615   to lend

1616   lens

The **leopard** is hunting.

1617   leopard

1618   leotard

There is **less** here.

1619

A **lesson** from the wise man

1620   lesson

1621   **Let** me go!

1622   letter of the alphabet

Ashley wrote this **letter.**

1623   letter

1624   lettuce

1625   **level** surface

1626   lever

You should never **lie.**

1627   liar

Be quiet, you are in the **library!**

1628   library

1629 licence plate/number plate*	**1630** to lick	The **lid** of the jar **1631** lid	I can tell if he is **lying**. **1632** to lie
This baby has just started his **life**. **1634** life	**1635** lifeboat	**1636** to lift	**1633** to lie down
1637 light/table lamp*	Dad **lights** the candle. **1638** to light	**1639** lightbulb	**1640** She **lightens** the load.
1641 lighthouse	**1642** lightning	**1643** lightning rod	Sharon **likes** her cat. **1644** to like
Sophie is not **likely** to come tomorrow. Ashley, that is a **likely** story! **1645** likely	**Lilacs** blossom in the spring. **1646** lilac	Easter **lilies** **1647** lily	The **limb** of a tree **1648** limb

1649   lime

There is a **limit** of three sweets for each child.

The speed **limit** is 30 miles per hour.

There is no **limit** to Joe's kindness.

1650   limit

Our neighbour walks with a **limp**.

1651   to limp

Can you draw a really straight **line**?

1652   line

1653   linen

An ocean **liner**

1654   liner

My jacket has a warm **lining**.

1655   lining

1656   to link

1657   lint

1658   lion

1659   lips

1660   lipstick

Water and milk are **liquids**.

1661   liquid

A **list** of things to do

1662   list

1663   They are **listening**.

A **litre** is a measure of volume.

1664   liter/litre*

Do not **litter**, ever!

1665   to litter

1666   a **little** apple

Ashley **lives** in the city.

Aunt Sally **lived** until she was seventy.

It would be difficult to **live** on the moon.

1667   to live

1668   lively

1669   living room/lounge*

1670   lizard

Tim is **loading** the cannon.

1671   to load

They are **loading** the truck.

1672   to load

A fresh **loaf** of bread

1673   loaf

Colin **lent** Ashley some money because she had spent her allowance.

1674   to loan/lend*

1675   lobster

Did you **lock** the door?

1676   to lock

1678   locomotive

1679   locust

A ski **chalet** in the mountains

1680   lodge/chalet*

There is a **lock** on the door.

1677   lock

1681   loft

1682   log

1683   lollipop

Eric is **lonely** because his friend has moved.

1684   lonely

The giraffe has a **long** neck.

1685   long

Frank **looks** longingly at the cakes.

1686   to look

Ashley weaves a scarf on her **loom**.

1687   loom

A **loop** in the rope

1688   loop

The strap is too **loose**.

1689   loose

Tony has **lost** a mitten.

1690   to **lose**

This **lotion** protects her skin.

1691   lotion

The **loud** music hurts Julia's ears.

1692   loud

1693   loudspeaker

1694   to **lounge**

Love is a very strong feeling.

Ashley says that if you have **love** you have everything.

1695   love

We **love** each other.

1696   to **love**

1697   lovely

1698   low branch

1699   to **lower**

Carl was very **lucky** to go on an adventure holiday.

Ashley is **lucky** to have such a cute little brother.

1700   lucky

Will all our clothes fit into the **luggage**?

1701   luggage

Lukewarm water is not hot and not cold.

1702   lukewarm water

Mum sings a **lullaby** to make the baby sleep.

1703   lullaby

1704   lumber/timber*

1705   lump

Susie is eating a sandwich for **lunch**.

1706   lunch

1707   lunchbox

Healthy **lungs** are important.

1708   lung

1709   magazine

1710   maggot

An unusual **magic** act.

1711   magic

1713   magnet

What a **magnificent** robe!

1714   magnificent

1715   magnifying glass

1712   magician

1716   magpie

1717   to **mail**/post*

1718 mail carrier/postman*

What is Gus **making**?

1719   to make

Melody wears **makeup**.

1720   makeup

Male and female

1721   male

1722   mallet

Man and woman

1723   man

A **mandarin** orange

1724   mandarin

Ashley's uncle plays the **mandolin**.

1725   mandolin

The **mane** is the hair on the horse's neck.

1726   mane

The **mango** is a very sweet fruit.

1727   mango

1728 He has good **manners.**

1729   many

1730   map

Making a **marble** statue
1731   marble

1733   to **march**

March is the third month of the year.
1734   March

A **mare** is a female horse.
1735   mare

1732   marbles

1736   marigold

Mark the right answer.
1737   to **mark**

You got excellent **marks.**
1738   mark

You can buy it at the **market.**
1739   market

1740   to **marry**

1741   marsh

Ashley always helps to **mash** the potatoes.
1742   to **mash** potatoes

It is only a **mask.**
1743   mask

1744   mass

Every sailing boat has a **mast.**
1745   mast

Andrea has **mastered** the art of bicycle riding.
1746   to **master**

A tennis **match**
1747   match

Never play with **matches**!

1748   match

1749   mathematics

What is the **matter** with Gordon?

1750   matter

1751   mattress

May is the fifth month of the year.

1752   May

Maybe Ashley should stay at home.

The answer is not yes, and it is not no, it is **maybe**.

1753   maybe

1754   mayor

Some people call it a labyrinth.

1755   maze

Meadows are covered with grass and flowers.

1756   meadow

1757   meadowlark

1758   meal

1759   mean person

May has **measles**.

1760   measles

Measure these lines with the ruler!

1761   to measure

1762   meat

1763   mechanic

Sara won a **medal** for bravery.

1764   medal

You must be careful with **medicine**.

1765   medicine

1766   medium

Fancy **meeting** you here!

1767   to meet

The teachers are in a **meeting**.

1768 meeting

1769 melon

1770 to **melt**

1771 Our club has four **members**.

1772 menu

We are at the **mercy** of the weather.

The bandits showed no **mercy** to their captives.

1773 mercy

1774 mermaid

1775 merry

1776 a real **mess**

There is an important **message** on this paper.

1777 message

The **messenger** is bringing the message.

1778 messenger

A mug made of **metal**

1779 metal

Meteorites come from outer space.

1780 meteorite

1781 meter

1 **metre** = about 40 inches

1782 meter/metre*

Ashley has a **method** for learning quickly.

A **method** is a way of doing things.

There is **method** to his madness.

1783 method

A **metronome** keeps rhythm.

1784 metronome

Terry sings into the **microphone**.

1785 microphone

1786 microscope

1787 microwave oven

1788 midday	1789 in the **middle**	1790 midget	1791 midnight

One **mile** equals 1.6 kilometres.

The speed limit is 30 **miles** per hour.

1792 mile	1793 milk	1794 mill	1795 mind

A brilliant **mind**

$E=MC^2$

The **mine** is deep underground. The **miner** checks the rock.

1796 mine	1797 miner	1798 minerals	1799 minnow

Sixty **minutes** in an hour

Something went wrong with this **miracle**.

1800 mint	1801 minus	1802 minute	1803 miracle

$7 - 5 = 2$

A **mirage** in the desert

Misers will not share.

Spud **misses** his family.

1804 mirage	1805 mirror	1806 miser	1807 to miss

1808 missile	Michael got lost in the **mist**. 1809 mist	1810 mistletoe	1811 mittens
1812 to mix	1813 mixer	The **moat** is full of water. 1814 moat	1815 to mock
1816 mockingbird	1817 model airplane/aeroplane*	1818 modern chair	He should not be smiling with a **moist** nappy! 1819 moist
1820 mole	A **mole** on my face. 1821 mole	Jane needs a **moment** to check her diary. 1822 One **moment** please.	**Monday** is the first day of the school week. Every **Monday**, Ashley gets up early. 1823 Monday
1824 money	1825 monkey	1826 monkfish	1827 monster

There are 12 **months** in a year. **1828** month	A **monument** to their leader **1829** monument
1830 He is in a good **mood.**	**1831** He is in a bad **mood.**
A crescent **moon** **1832** moon	**1833** moose
Time to get up! **1834** morning	**1835** **mortar** and pestle
1836 mosaic	**1837** mosquito
Moss sometimes grows on tree trunks. **1838** moss	**1839** mother
An electric **motor** **1840** motor	**1841** motorcycle
A jelly **mould** **1842** mould*/mold	A **mound** of earth **1843** mound
He **mounts** his horse to go to work. **1844** to mount	**1845** mountain
1846 mouse	**1847** moustache*/mustache

1848 mouth

Snails **move** slowly.

1849 to move

Movement from side to side

1850 movement

1851 movie/film*

1852 to **mow** the lawn

1853 too **much** for me

Why is he sitting in the **mud**?

1854 mud

1855 mule

1856 multiply

Being ill with **mumps** makes your face swell.

1857 mumps

To **murder** someone is an awful crime.

1858 to murder

1859 muscle

You can find rare things in a **museum**.

1860 museum

Some **mushrooms** are poisonous.

1861 mushroom

Ashley loves **music**.

1862 music

Ashley's Mum is a **musician**.

1863 musician

Mussels live in the sea and have hard shells.

1864 mussel

1865 You **must** jump.

1866 mustard

1867 muzzle

N

1868 nail

1869 finger**nail**

1870 **nail** clipper

1872 **naked**

What is your **name**?

1873 My **name** is…

1874 **napkin**/serviette*

1871 to **nail**

1875 too **narrow** to pass

A tiny **nation**!

1876 **nation**

It is healthy to eat **natural** foods.

Raisins are a **natural** source of energy.

He has not dyed his hair - that is its **natural** colour.

1877 **natural**

Nature is beautiful.

1878 **nature**

1879 She is **naughty**.

Captain Jones **navigates** by the stars.

1880 to **navigate**

She is getting **near**.

1881 **near**

1882 **neat**

1883 Not pleasant, but **necessary**.

1884 **neck**

1885 **necklace**

Bees use **nectar** to make honey.

1886 **nectar**

1887   nectarine

A friend in **need** is a friend indeed.

There is a great **need** for water in the desert.

1888   need

1889   I **need** water.

Can you thread a **needle**?

1890   needle

Neglected dogs can get fleas.

1891   He **neglects** his dog.

The horse **neighs** to wake up Ashley.

1892   to neigh

1893   neighbors/neighbours*

Neither shoe is right.

1894   **neither** one fits

This **neon sign** lights up the front of a petshop.

1895   neon sign

1896   My **nephew** is my brother's son.

There are many **nerves** in your body.

1897   nerve

Ron is so **nervous**, he never relaxes.

1898   nervous

Two eggs in the **nest**

1899   nest

Nettles can sting.

1900   nettle

Never, ever!

1901   **Never** play with fire!

1902   new

Mum reads the **news.**

The **news** is good.

Any **news** from home?

1903   news

1904   newspaper

You are **next**.

1905   **Next** !

The squirrel **nibbles** on a nut.

1906   to nibble

One of them is a **nice** child.

1907　　nice

Nickel is a kind of metal, often used to make coins.

1908　　nickel

Her name is Ashley, but her **nickname** is Spots.

1909　　nickname

Ashley is Samantha's **niece**.

1910　My **niece** is my brother's daughter.

Owls hunt at **night**.

1911　　night

1912　　nightingale

A **nightmare** is a bad dream.

1913　　nightmare

1914　　nine

The answer is **NO**.

1916　　no

Sir Galahad is **noble** and generous.

Helping that old lady across the street was a **noble** deed.

1917　　noble

1918　　nobleman

1915　　ninth

There is **nobody** sitting here.

1919　　nobody

A loud **noise**

1920　　noise

Twelve o'clock **noon**

1921　　noon

1922　　north

There is a fly on my **nose**!

1923　　nose

1924　　nuts

1925　　nutcracker

1926　nylon stockings/**tights***

1927 oak

That shark must like **oars**!

1928 oar

An **oasis** in the desert

1929 oasis

An **oblong** object is longer than it is wide.

1930 oblong

1931 to observe

Ships sail across the **ocean**.

1932 ocean

An **octagon** has eight sides.

1933 octagon

The tenth month of the year

1934 October

1935 octopus

A **milometer** tells you how far you have travelled.

1936 odometer/milometer*

1937 odor/odour*

Please get **off** that chair.

This food tastes **off**.

Off we go into the mountains.

The light is **off**.

1938 off

He **offers** money for the cow.

1939 to offer

1940 officer

Ashley **often** asks difficult questions.

How **often** does the train run?

Often enough!

1941 often

1942 oil

1943 ointment

A very **old** man

1944 old

Olives grow on trees.

1945 olive

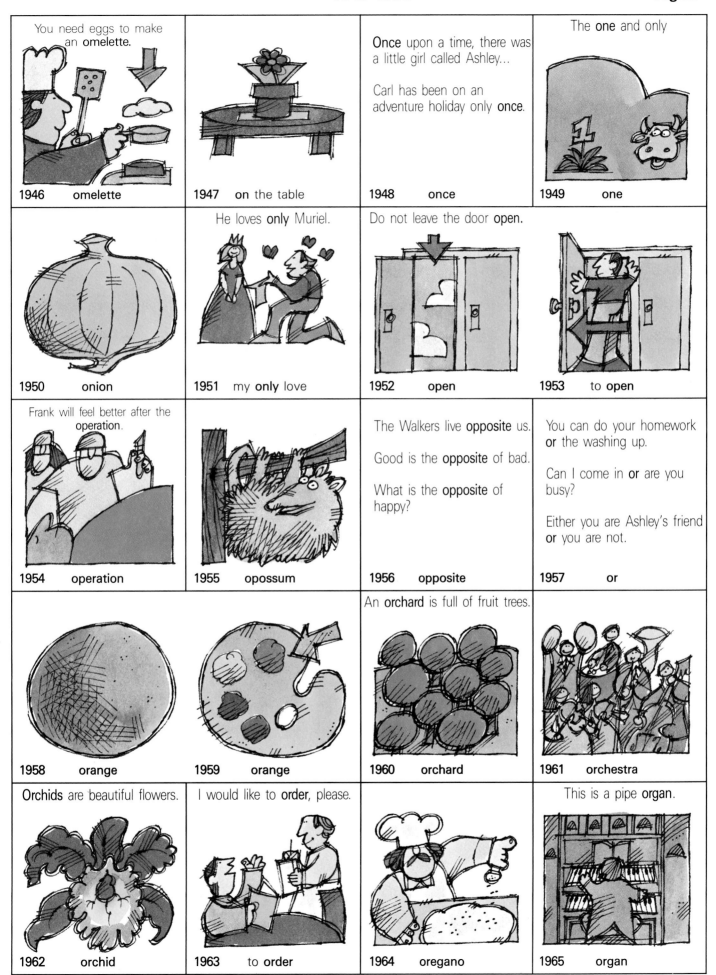

You need eggs to make an **omelette**.

1946 omelette

1947 **on** the table

Once upon a time, there was a little girl called Ashley...

Carl has been on an adventure holiday only **once**.

1948 once

The **one** and only

1949 one

1950 onion

He loves **only** Muriel.

1951 my **only** love

Do not leave the door **open**.

1952 open

1953 to **open**

Frank will feel better after the **operation**.

1954 operation

1955 opossum

The Walkers live **opposite** us.

Good is the **opposite** of bad.

What is the **opposite** of happy?

1956 opposite

You can do your homework **or** the washing up.

Can I come in **or** are you busy?

Either you are Ashley's friend **or** you are not.

1957 or

1958 orange

1959 orange

An **orchard** is full of fruit trees.

1960 orchard

1961 orchestra

Orchids are beautiful flowers.

1962 orchid

I would like to **order**, please.

1963 to order

1964 oregano

This is a pipe **organ**.

1965 organ

	An **orphan** has no parents.	The **ostrich** cannot fly.	**Otters** eat fish.
1966 oriole	1967 orphan	1968 ostrich	1969 otter

Sixteen **ounces** to the pound	The great **outdoors**	Do you like my **outfit**?	
1970 ounce	1971 outdoors	1972 outfit	1973 oval

An apple pie is baking in the **oven**.			
1974 oven	1975 Man **overboard**!	1976 overcoat	1977 to **overflow**

		You **owe** respect to your teacher. It is best not to **owe** any money.	
1978 overshoe	1979 to **overturn**	1980 to **owe**	1981 owl

We **own** our house, we do not rent it. Ashley **owns** 2 pairs of shoes.			This **oyster** has a pearl inside.
1982 to **own**	1983 ox	1984 oxygen	1985 oyster

P

Ashley **packs** her bag.

1986   to **pack**

1987   package

Someone wrote on my **pad** of paper.

1988   pad

Sharon is holding her **paddle**.

1990   paddle

1991   to **paddle**

1992   padlock

A launch **pad**

1989   pad

Please turn the **page**.

1993   page

A **pail** of water is very heavy.

1994   pail

1996   paint

It is not a good idea to touch **wet paint**.

1997   wet **paint**

Tom has hurt his finger and is in **pain**.

1995   pain

2000   painter

Aunt Polly told Tom to **paint** the fence.

1998   to **paint**

1999   paintbrush

2001   painting

2002   a **pair** of shoes

2003   palace

The colour of this flower is rather **pale**.

2004   pale

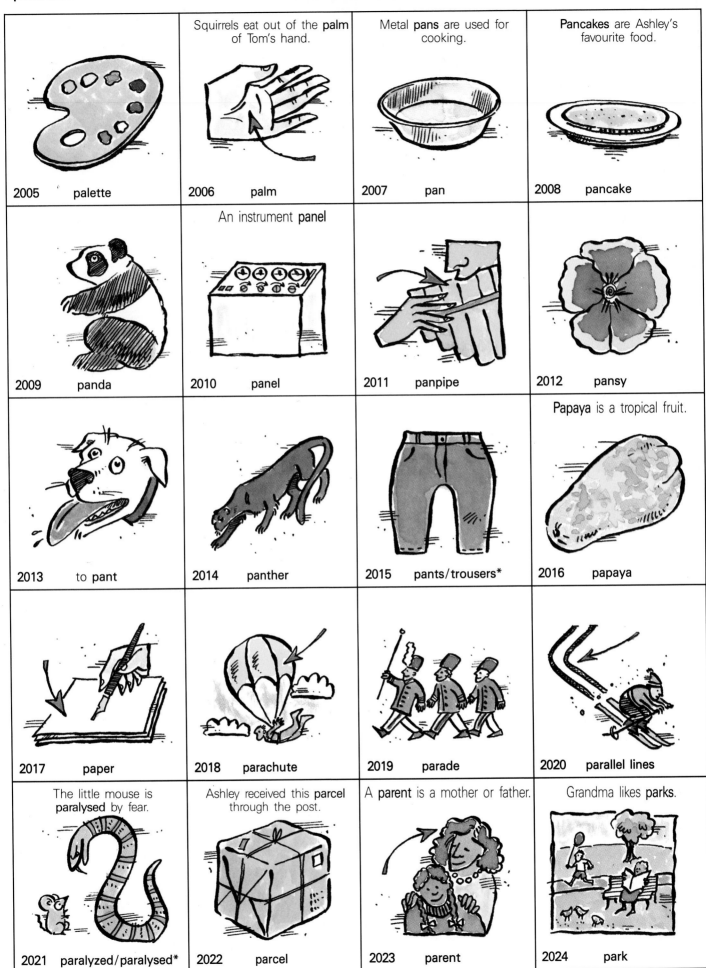

2005 palette	Squirrels eat out of the **palm** of Tom's hand. 2006 palm	Metal **pans** are used for cooking. 2007 pan	**Pancakes** are Ashley's favourite food. 2008 pancake
2009 panda	An instrument **panel** 2010 panel	2011 panpipe	2012 pansy
2013 to pant	2014 panther	2015 pants/trousers*	**Papaya** is a tropical fruit. 2016 papaya
2017 paper	2018 parachute	2019 parade	2020 parallel lines
The little mouse is **paralysed** by fear. 2021 paralyzed/paralysed*	Ashley received this **parcel** through the post. 2022 parcel	A **parent** is a mother or father. 2023 parent	Grandma likes **parks**. 2024 park

Ashley's Dad always **parks** the car here.

2025   to park

Emily's **parka** keeps her warm in winter.

2026   parka

The Houses of **Parliament**

2027   parliament

This **parrot** repeats every word you say.

2028   parrot

Parsley is a kind of herb.

2029   parsley

2030   parsnip

Dust **particles** fly in the air.

2031   particle

Charlie is a good dancing partner.

2032   partner

Ashley loves **parties**.

2033   party

Mary **passed** the ball...   ...but Joe **passed** out.

2034   to pass   2035   to pass out

2036   passage

2037   passenger

You need a **passport** to travel abroad.

2038   passport

In the **past**, there were no planes or cars.

It is now **past** Ashley's bedtime.

Tom drove **past** our house.

2039   past

Pasta includes spaghetti and macaroni.

2040   pasta

Jim **pastes** up wallpaper.

2041   to paste

Needlework is her favourite pastime.

2042   pastime

Cakes and biscuits are **pastries**.

2043   pastry

Sheep graze in the **pasture**.

2044   pasture

A **patch** where it counts

2045   patch

2046   path

Ashley is not sleeping, she is waiting for her brother.

2047   She is **patient**.

One worried **patient**

2048   patient

A dress **pattern**

2049   pattern

After reading two pages, Ashley **paused** for a few seconds.

I have to **pause** for breath.

2050   to pause

2051   pavement/road*

How many **paws** does a cat have?

2052   paw

Your parents have to **pay** a lot of bills.

2053   to ´pay

2054 pay phone/phone box*

Peace on Earth

2055   peace

2056   peach

2057   peacock

2058   peak

2059   peal of a bell

2060   peanut

2061   pear

A **pearl** in the oyster

2062   pearl

Peas in a pod

2063   peas

Peat moss helps plants grow.

2064   peat moss

Pebbles on the beach

2065   pebbles

A **pecan** is a nut.

2066   pecan

2067   to peck

2068   pedal

2070   pedestrian

It is safer to cross the road at a zebra crossing.

2071   pedestrian crossing

2072   to peel

2069   to pedal

2073   pelican

2074   pen

2075   pencil

A **pendulum** clock

2076   pendulum

2077   penguin

The blade of a **penknife** folds away when not in use.

2078   penknife

A **pentagon** has five sides.

2079   pentagon

Many happy **people**

2080   people

A **pepper** mill

2081   pepper

2082   peppermint

2083   perch

A bird on its **perch**

2084   perch

A great **performance**

2085   performance

2086   perfume

The **full stop** comes at the end of a sentence.

2087   period/full stop*

2088   periwinkle

Tom is a young male **person**.

2089   person

2090   pest

Burt **pesters** his dad.

2091   to pester

My **pet** snake

2092   pet

Flowers have **petals**.

2094   petal

2095   petunia

The hospital **pharmacist** makes up the prescripton.

2096   pharmacist/chemist*

The baby **pets** the dog.

2093   to pet

2097   pharmacy/chemist's*

2098   pheasant

Phone or telephone

2099   phone

2100   photograph

2101   piano

Pick a card!

2102   to pick

Emily **picks up** the doll.

2103   to pick up

2104   pickaxe

Vinegar is used in making **pickles**.

2105   pickles

Ashley knows how to **pickle** vegetables.

2106   to pickle

2107   picnic

Pablo's **pictures** are strange.

2108   picture

Pecan **pie**...

2109   pie

Mmmm!

2110   a piece/slice* of pie

2111   to piece together

A **pier** by the sea

2112   pier

2113   pig

2114   pigeon

A real **pigsty**

2115   pigsty

A **pile** of earth

2116   pile

Pills can be very dangerous.

2117   pill/tablet*

2118   pillar

Cats love **pillows**.

2119   pillow

2120   pillowcase

Every aeroplane needs a **pilot**.

2121   pilot

2122   pimple

2123   pincers

Pinching can hurt.

2124   to pinch

2125 pine

Pineapples do not grow on pine trees.

2126 pineapple

2127 pink

2128 pipe

2129 pirate

2130 pistachio

A very old **pistol**

2131 pistol

Merv **pitches** the baseball.

2132 to **pitch**

Ashley **pities** the poor boy who lost his cat.

What a **pity** ....

2136 to **pity**

There is no **place** like home.

Would you like to come to our **place**?

Try to keep everything in **place**!

2137 place

2138 plaice

Hey Merv, that was a good **pitch**!

This song is off **pitch**.

Salesmen like to make a **pitch.**

2133 pitch

2139 **plain** shirt

The **plain** stretches for hundreds of miles.

2140 plain

2141 to **plan**

2134 pitchfork

This **plane** belongs to a carpenter.

2142 plane

Planets around the sun

2143 planets

2144 plank

2135 pitch tar

2145   plants   2146   to plant

Pam **plasters** the wall.

2147   plaster   2148   to plaster

Many household objects are made of **plastic**.

2149   plastic

2150   plasticine

This is Ashley's dinner **plate**.

2151   plate

2152   plateau

The train is at the **platform**.

2153   platform

Children **play** together in the **playground**.

2154   to play   2155   playground

2156   playing cards

Please spare my life, I beg of you!

2157   to **plead**

2158   a **pleasant** day

2159   A glass of milk, **please**.

This kilt has many **pleats**.

2160   pleat

2161   pliers

2162   plow/plough*

2163   to pluck

2164   plug

2165   plug

2166   plum

2167   plumber

2168   plump

'One' is singular, 'many' is **plural**.

Children is the **plural** of child.

2169   plural

One **plus** one equals...

2170   plus

2171   plywood

Jacques **poaches** some eggs.

2172   to **poach**

2173   pocket

2174   pea **pod**

A **poem** has sets of words that rhyme,
A poet writes **poems** and has a good time.

2175   poem

It is not polite to **point**.

2177   to **point**

2176   poinsettia

2180   poison

Some insects have a **poisonous** sting.

There are not many **poisonous** snakes.

2181   poisonous

A very sharp **point**

2178   point

If you **poke** me in the back, I get very cross.

2182   to **poke**

2183   polar bear

2184   pole

2179   pointed

2185 policeman

2186 policewoman

Henry **polishes** the cup until it shines.

2187 to polish

Everybody likes **polite** children.

It is not **polite** to shout.

The teacher expects a **polite** answer.

2188 polite

Pollen gives some people hayfever.

2189 pollen

2190 pomegranate

2191 pond

Susie rides her **pony** every morning.

2192 pony

Fun at the swimming **pool**

2193 pool

We **pool** our resources.

2194 to pool

Ashley had **poor** results because she did not work hard.

Her family is not **poor**, but it is not rich either.

2195 poor

2196 to pop

2197 poplar

2198 poppy

Ashley is a **popular** girl.

This book is very **popular**.

2199 popular

Ron sits on the **porch**.

2200 porch

2201 **Pores** are little holes in the skin.

Porridge for breakfast

2202 porridge

2203 port

Ashley wants a **portable** radio, but she has not saved up enough money from her allowance.

Susie watches her **portable** TV in the garden.

2204 portable

The **porter** carries Aunt Vera's luggage.

2205   porter

This is a **portrait** of Aunt Vera.

2206   portrait

2207   post

Peter **posts** a letter to Aunt Vera.

2208   to **post**

Aunt Vera sends a **postcard** to Peter.

2210   postcard

2211   poster

2212   pot

2209   post office

2213   potato

2214   pottery

Do you keep your coins in a **pouch**?

2215   pouch

2216   to **pounce**

Four bananas weigh about a **pound**.

One **pound** is quite a lot of money in England.

2217   pound

2218   to **pound**

2219   to **pour**

2220   to **pout**

Eric puts on talcum **powder** after his bath.

2221   powder

2222   to **practice/practise***

Wheat grows on the **prairies**.

2223   prairie

Good show, children!

2224   to **praise**

The horse **prances** about.

2225   to **prance**

2226   to **pray**

I **prefer** that one.

2227   to **prefer**

Her baby is expected next month.

2228   She is **pregnant.**

2229   I am **present.**

2230   birthday **present**

Bob **presents** the trophy.

2231   to **present**

2232   **preserved** fruit

Press the button to call the lift.

2233   to **press**

2234   **pretty**

The owl caught its **prey.**

2235   **prey**

2236   **price**

2237   to **prick**

2238   **prickly** animal

2239   **primary** school

2240   **primrose**

2241   **prince**

2242   **princess**

2243   school **principal/**Head teacher*

In **principle**, I agree with you.

The first **principle** is hard work.

Truth is a sacred **principle.**

2244   **principle**

2245   to **print**

Light becomes a rainbow when it passes through a **prism**.

2246   prism

Spud went to **prison** for his crimes.

2247   prison

2248   prisoner

Ashley and I are having a **private** talk.

Tom takes **private** lessons.

He is a very **private** person.

2249   private

Ashley won first **prize** in swimming this year.

2250   prize

2251   problem

Fresh farm **produce**

2252   produce

There are not many good television **programmes**.

2254   program/programme*

2255   prohibited

Shirley is working on a **project**.

Ashley did not do well on her **project**.

2256   project

2253 This factory **produces** cars.

Boy scouts **promise** to be good.

2257   I promise.

This pitchfork has four **prongs**.

2258   prong

Pronounce your words carefully.

2259   to pronounce

Proof that Tigger ate the bird

2260   proof of guilt

Emma **props** up the board.

2261   to prop

2262   propeller

2263   properly dressed

Ashley says "This is mine" when she means "This is my **property**".

Her family owns **property** in the country.

2264   property

2265   to **protest**

2266   I am a **proud** cat.

I can **prove** it, Sir.

2267   to **prove**

Here is a **proverb**:

"An apple a day keeps the doctor away."

2268   proverb

2269   to **provide** chairs

A **prune** is a dried plum.

2270   prune

2271   to **prune**

2272   public telephone/**phone box***

Pudding for dessert

2273   pudding/**afters***

2274   puddle

2275   to **puff**

2276   puffin

2277   to **pull**

2278   pulley

2279   pullover/**sweater***

The doctor takes Ashley's **pulse**.

2280   pulse

2281   pump

2282   to **pump**

2283   pumpkin

2284   to **punch**

You have arrived on time.

2285 You are **punctual.**

Tom will be punished for **puncturing** the tyre.

2286 to **puncture**

2287 to **punish**

2288 **punishment**

A **puppet** like Pinocchio

2289 **puppet**

2290 **puppy**

2291 **pure** water

2292 **purple**

Cats **purr** when they are happy.

2293 to **purr**

2294 **purse/handbag***

2295 to **pursue**

2296 to **push**

Put it here, please.

2297 to **put**

2298 to **put away**

Tim **puts off** reading until later.

2299 to **put off**

Putty keeps the window pane in place.

2300 **putty**

2301 **puzzle**

2302 **pyjamas*/pajamas**

2303 **pyramid**

2304 **python**

2305   quail

2306   **quality** watch

Ashley says "amount" when she means "**quantity**".

2307   quantity

2308   to **quarrel**

There are stone **quarries** and sand **quarries**.

2309   quarry

2310   quarter

A boat docked at the **quay**.

2311   quay

2312   queen

2313   to ask a **question**

Be **quick** about it!

2314   quick

He is sinking in **quicksand**.

2315   quicksand

2316   She is **quiet**.

A **quill** is a feather used as a pen.

2317   quill

2318   porcupine **quill**

2319   quilt/eiderdown*

2320   quince

A **quiver** full of arrows

2321   quiver

2322   to **quiver**

Our class had a **quiz** in spelling today.

2323   quiz

R

2324 rabbit

2325 raccoon

2326 to race

2327 rack/hat-stand*

Terry makes a **racket**.

2328 racket

2329 radiator

2330 radio

2331 radish

The **radius** of a circle

2332 radius

2333 raft

2334 a **raid** in progress

Hold on to the hand**rail**.

2335 hand**rail/banister***

2336 railroad track/railway track*

It is **raining** cats and dogs.

2337 to rain

Ashley loves to watch **rainbows**.

2338 rainbow

2339 raincoat

All those who like Ashley, **raise** your hands!

She has **raised** an interesting question.

2340 to raise

Raisins are dried grapes.

2341 raisin

2342 rake

Billy **raps** on the door.
2343   to rap/knock*

2344   rapid

2345   rare

A **rash** on his face
2346   rash

2347   raspberry

2348   rat

2349   rattle

2350   rattlesnake

2351   raven

2352   ravenous

2353   ravine

2354   a raw egg

2355   ray of sunlight

2356   razor

2357   to reach

2358   to read

On your marks...**ready**...
2359   ready

Is this a **real** diamond?
2360   real

2361   to realize/realise*

Kathy is **really** happy.
2362   Are you **really** here?

2363   rear

2364   rearview mirror

John tries to **reason** with the examiner.

2365   to reason

That is a **reasonable** price.

Ashley, please be **reasonable**.

2366   reasonable

People do **rebel** against high taxes.

Spartacus **rebelled** against Rome.

2367   to rebel

2368   I do not **recall.**

Sally has just **received** a gift.

2369   to receive

2370   recently hatched

2371   recipe

Can you **recite** a poem?

2372   to recite

2373   record

2374   record player

Ashley scraped her knee but she will **recover** quickly.

I **recovered** all the books that were left outside.

2375   to recover

2376   rectangle

2377   red

2378   reed

A coral **reef**

2379   reef

Something in there really **reeks.**

2380   to reek

The line is wound on the **reel.**

2381   reel

2382   referee

2383   reflection

Never leave the **refrigerator** door open.

2384   refrigerator

2385   to refuse

This **region** of the country is crossed by rivers.

2386   region

2387   to register

Tom **regrets** what happened.

2388   to regret

2389   Actors **rehearse** a play.

2390   reindeer

2391   reins

2392   relatives

2393   to relax

2394   to release

2395   **Remember** to brush your teeth.

2396   remote island

Phil **removes** his hat.

2397   to remove

We **rent** a flat.

If you do not have a car, you can **rent** one.

2398   to rent

2399   to repair

The parrot **repeats** every word.

2400   to repeat

2401   to replace

He asked and she **replied**.

2402   to reply

	Jim **rescues** the cat.	Water is stored in a **reservoir**.	Ashley, you are **responsible** for your little brother Carl. Dad saw the milk spilled on the floor and said:"Who is **responsible** for this?"
2403 reptile	2404 to **rescue**	2405 reservoir	2406 responsible
		Ashley always **returns** her library books. John is away from home, but he will **return** soon.	
2407 to **rest**	2408 restaurant	2409 to **return**	2410 reverse
		Here is a **rhyme** for you: Hickory dickory dock, The mouse ran up the clock. The clock struck one, The mouse ran down, Hickory dickory dock.	
2411 rhinoceros	2412 rhubarb	2413 rhyme	2414 rib
Can you make a bow with **ribbon**?	A bowl of **rice**	The ribbon is a **rich** red colour. The **rich** must always help the poor.	Nobody can solve this **riddle**.
2415 ribbon	2416 rice	2417 rich	2418 riddle
			Turn **right** at the corner. It is not **right** to steal. Ashley thinks she is always **right**. Hold it the **right** way up.
2419 to **ride** a horse	2420 ridge	2421 my **right** hand	2422 right

2423 right-handed	The sausage has a tough **rind**. 2424 rind	2425 ring	Uncle Sam **rings** the doorbell. 2426 to ring
An ice hockey **rink** 2427 rink	Ashley's dad **rinses** the dishes. 2428 to rinse	2429 riot	You must have **ripped** your trousers! 2430 to rip
This apple is ready to eat. 2431 ripe	2432 ripple	The sun **rises**. 2433	Always be careful when taking **risks**. The weather forecaster said there was a **risk** of frost. 2434 risk
2435 rivals	2436 river	2437 road	The lion **roars** to impress Mr. Tamer. 2438 to roar
A nice **roast** straight from the oven. 2439 roast	**Robbers** are criminals. 2440 robber	2441 robin	2442 rock

| 2443   to rock | 2444   rocket | 2445   rocking chair | 2446   rod |
| 2447   roll | 2448   to roll | 2449   roller skate | 2450   rolling pin |

Our house has a tile **roof**.

Hens **roost** at night.

| 2451   roof | 2452   room | 2453   to roost | 2454   root |

Karen has **rosy** cheeks.

| 2455   rope | 2456   rose | 2457   rosemary | 2458   rosy |

A rather **rough** beard

| 2459   **rotten** apple | 2460   rough | 2461   round | 2462   4 buttons in a **row** |

She **rows** faster than Michael.

2463   to **row**

The king is part of the **royal** family.

2464   **royal**

Tyres and balls are made of **rubber**.

2465   **rubber**

2466   **rubbish**

2467   **ruby**

A **rudder** is used for steering.

2468   **rudder**

2469   He is **rude**.

This is difficult country to walk through.

2470   **rugged** terrain

The **ruins** of an ancient castle

2471   **ruin**

Some countries are under the **rule** of a king.

Ashley seldom breaks the **rules**.

Mum and Dad make the **rules** in this house.

2472   **rule**

The king is the **ruler**.

2473   **ruler**

2474   I hear a **rumble**.

Can he **run** faster than a speeding bullet?

2475   to **run**

2476   to **run away**

2477   to **run over**

2478   to **run out** of energy

She **rushed** to catch it, but it was too late.

2479   to **rush**

Iron man has **rust** everywhere.

2480   **rust**

The car is stuck in a **rut**.

2481   **rut**

2482   **rye**

A **sack** of flour

2483 sack

2484 Truth is a **sacred** principle.

2485 sad

What is inside the **safe**?

2486 saddle

2487 safe

2488 sail

2489 sailboard

It is going cheap in the **sale**.

2490 sailboat/sailing boat*

2491 sailor

2492 salad

2493 sale

Salt and pepper

2494 salmon

2495 salt

2496 to salute

2497 same

Ashley can make her own **sandwich**.

2498 sand

2499 sandal

2500 sandwich

2501 sap

Many **sardines** in a can

2502   sardine

We receive TV pictures by **satellite**.

2503   satellite

Satin is smooth and shiny.

2504   satin dress

The weekend starts on **Saturday**.

Saturday is play day.

Ashley likes **Saturdays**.

2505   Saturday

2506   sauce/gravy*

2507   sausage

I **save** my money.

2508   I **save** my money.

This **saw** is very sharp.

2509   saw

2511   sawdust

2512   I **say** what I think.

The **scaffolding** supports the artist.

2513   scaffolding

2510   to **saw**

Careful not to **scald** yourself!

2514   to **scald**

One side is heavier.

2515   scale

Scallops are very tasty.

2516   scallop

2517   scalp

The man with the **scar**

2518   scar

She likes to **scare** him.

2519   to **scare**

Scarecrows are for the birds.

2520   scarecrow

A very warm **scarf**

2521   scarf

2522   scarlet

The police are at the **scene**.

2523   **scene** of a crime

2524   scenery

Scholarship means learning.

2525   scholarship

This is the **school** Ashley goes to.

2526   school

2527   schooner

2528   scissors

2529   to scoop

2530   scooter

The paper is not quite burnt.

2531   scorched paper

2532   to score

2533   scout

2534   scraps of paper

I always **scrape** my knees.

2535   scrape

2536   scraper

2537   scratch

2538   screen

2539   screw

2540   screwdriver

Wally **scrubs** the floor.

2541   to scrub

2542 sculptor	2543 seahorse	There is a lot of water in the **sea**. 2544 Adriatic **sea**	2545 seagull
2546 seal	2547 seam	What is Harry looking for? 2548 to **search**	2549 searchlight
The four **seasons** are: Spring Summer Autumn Winter 2550 seasons	2551 seat	Ashley has fastened her **seatbelt**. 2552 seatbelt	2553 seaweed
2554 second	Ashley knows how to keep a **secret**. 2555 I have a **secret**.	2556 to **see**	2557 see-saw
The **seed** grows into a new plant. 2558 seed	Later, the bird revived. 2559 It **seems** to be dead.	2560 to **seize**	Ashley does not like **selfish** kids. 2561 You are **selfish**.

Jessica **sells** fruit in her shop.

2562 to **sell**

2563 **semicircle**

Michael **sent** his cousin a birthday present.

2564 to **send**

Karen's skin is **sensitive** to the sun.

2565 **sensitive** skin

Can you make a **sentence**?

The robber received a prison **sentence**.

2566 **sentence**

2567 **sentry**

September is the ninth month of the year.

2568 **September**

The butler **serves** dinner to the duchess.

2569 to **serve**

2570 **seven**

2571 **seventh**

2572 **several**

2573 to **sew**

2574 **sewing machine**

Although it is **shabby**, it is my favourite chair.

2575 **shabby**

2576 **shack**

2577 **shadow**

A **shaggy** dog

2578 **shaggy**

2579 to **shake**

2580 **shallow** water

Mum washes her hair with **shampoo**.

2581 **shampoo**

We can **share** it.

2582   to **share**

Is this **shark** learning how to fly?

2583   **shark**

2584   **sharp**

2585   knife **sharpener**

The glass **shattered**.

2588   to **shatter**

2589   to **shave**

2590   **shears**

2586   skate **sharpener**

2591   **sheath**

Ashley counts **sheep** before falling asleep.

2592   **sheep**

Tuck in the **sheet** when you make the bed.

2593   **sheet**

2587   pencil **sharpener**

2594   **shelf**

2595   **shell**

The leaf is the beetle's **shelter**.

2596   **shelter**

2597   **shepherd**

2598   **shield**

2599   **shin**

The sun **shines** brightly.

2600   to **shine**

2601   **shingle**

Shingles is a disease.

2602   shingles

2603   shiny

2604   ship

2605   shipwreck

2606   shirt

2607   to shiver

Avoid electric **shocks**!

2608   shock

2609   shoes

2610   shoelace

2611   shoemaker

2612   to shoot

2613   shop

2614   shopkeeper

2615   shop window

The water starts at the **shore**.

2616   shore

2617   short

2618   shorts

2619   shoulder

2620   to shout

It is very rude to **shove** people.

2621   to shove

A snow **shovel**

2622   shovel

2623   to show

2624   to show off

2625   to show up/appear*

Curtis takes a **shower.**

2626   shower

2627   to shriek

2628   shrimp

2629   to shrink

2630   shrub

Mr. Fast **shuffles** the cards.

2631   shuffle

The **shutters** are closed at night.

2632   shutters

2633   shy

2634   sick

There are no windows on this **side.**

2635   side

Always walk on the **pavement.**

2636   sidewalk/pavement*

A heavy **sigh**

2637   to sigh

2638   sign

2639   to signal

2640   signature

Ashley is not **silent** very often.

A **silent** night is a quiet night.

2641   silent

The window **sill**

2642   sill

Jonathan thinks Ashley is **silly**.

Ashley thinks Jonathan does **silly** things.

2643   silly

Silver is a precious metal.

2644   silver

That is the truth, pure and **simple**.

There is a **simple** solution.

2645   simple

2646   to sing

'One' is **singular**.

'Several' is plural.

2647   singular

2648   sink

Sink or swim!

2649   to sink

Marg is **sipping** her drink.

2650   to sip

2651   siren

My **sister** and I have the same parents.

2652   sister

2653   to sit

2654   six

2655   sixth

Does it come in my **size**?

2656   size

2657   to skate

2658   skateboard

What is a **skeleton** doing in my cupboard?

2659   skeleton

2660   to sketch

2661   skis

	Horace almost **skidded** off the path.		
2662 to **ski**	2663 to **skid**	2664 **skin**	2665 to **skip**
2666 **skipper/captain***	2667 **skirt**	2668 **skull**	There are clouds in the **sky**. 2669 **sky**
2670 **skylark**	A **skyscraper** is a very tall building. 2671 **skyscraper**	He **slammed** the door. 2672 to **slam**	2673 **slanting** floor
2674 to **slap**	Zorro is **slashing** around again. 2675 to **slash**	Paul writes on the **slate** with chalk. 2676 **slate**	2677 **sled/sleigh***
Zorro is **sleeping**. 2678 to **sleep**	A **sleeping bag** for camping. 2679 **sleeping bag**	Paul feels **sleepy**. 2680 **sleepy**	I wish this **sleet** would turn to proper snow. 2681 **sleet**

			A **slimy** creature
2682 sleeve	2683 slide	2684 slim	2685 slimy
His arm is in a **sling**.			
2686 sling	2687 slingshot/catapult*	2688 to slip	2689 slipper
	What a **slob**!		
2690 slippery	2691 slob	2692 slope	2693 slot
You must not **slouch**.	The car **slows down** at the corner. **Slow down**, Dad! You are going too fast. Nothing can **slow** Ashley **down**.		
2694 to slouch	2695 to slow down	2696 slush	2697 small
That was a **smart** thing to do. She is wearing a **smart** dress.	Do not **smash** the watch!		Hector **smells** the flower.
2698 smart/clever*	2699 to smash	2700 to smear	2701 to smell

What a **smelly** skunk!

2702   smelly

People who **smoke** are like skunks.

2703   to **smoke**

The ice Ashley is skating on is very **smooth**.

A good aeroplane pilot makes **smooth** landings.

2704   smooth

2705   to have a **snack**

2706   snail

2707   snake

2708   to **snap**

2709   sneakers/trainers*

The dust made her **sneeze.**

2710   to **sneeze**

2711   snorkel

2712   snow

2713   snowflake

2714   snowshoes

Wash with **soap** and water!

2715   soap

They call it **soccer** in America but football in England.

2716   soccer

2717   sock

2718   socket

2719   sofa/couch*

Soft and cuddly

2720   soft

2721   soldier

2722 sole	2723 She **solves** the problem.	2724 to **somersault**	2725 son
2726 song	**Soon** it will be dark. Ashley will be home **soon**. She **soon** got tired of her new doll. 2727 soon	2728 sorcerer	2729 My arm is **sore**.
Sorrel is very tasty. 2730 sorrel	Grover is truly **sorry**. 2731 sorry	2732 to **sort**	2733 soup
2734 sour	2735 south	The **sow** is the mother of the piglets. 2736 sow	The farmer **sows** the seed on the field. 2737 to **sow**
2738 spaceship	2739 spade	2740 to **spank**	Every car must have a **spare** tyre. 2741 **spare** tire/tyre*

2742 spark	Her rings **sparkle** in the sun. **2743** to **sparkle**	**2744** sparrow	They both **speak** English. **2745** to **speak**
2746 spear	The turtle is slow even when it **speeds up**. **2747** to **speed up**	Alice is about to **spell** her name. **2748** to **spell**	**2749** to **spend**
A **sphere** is round. **2750** sphere	Hot and **spicy** **2751** spicy	The **spider** spins a web. **2752** spider	**2753** spike
2754 to **spill**	**2755** to **spin**	**Spinach** is one of my favourite vegetables. **2756** spinach	Also called the backbone **2757** spine
2758 spiral	**2759** spire	No polite person ever **spits**. **2760** to **spit**	**2761** to **splash**

There are **splinters** everywhere.

2762   splinter

2763 spoiled/rotten* fruit

2764   sponge

2765   spool/reel*

2766   spoon

How did that **spot** get there?

2767   spot

2768   spout

Ashley **sprained** her ankle.

2769   to sprain

2770   to spray

2771   to spread

2772   spring

Spring is here at last.

2773   spring

2775   to sprinkle

She **sprints** to win.

2776   to sprint

2777   spruce

The **spring** runs swiftly.

2774   spring

2778   square

2779   squash

2780   to squat

Ashley **squeezes** and hugs her friend.

2781   to squeeze

2782   squid

2783   squirrel

2784   to squirt

The horses are in the **stable**.

2785   stable

A dancer on **stage**

2786   stage

2787   stain

2788   staircase

2789   wooden stake

Stale bread is dry and hard.

2790   **stale** bread

2791   celery **stalk**

A **stallion** is a male horse.

2792   stallion

2793   stamp

2794   to stand

Twinkle, twinkle little **star**!

2795   star

Ashley is **staring** at you.

2796   to stare

2797   starling

2798   to **start** a car

When Ashley says "I'm **starving**", she means that she is hungry.

You will not **starve**, Ashley!

2799   to starve

2800   gas/petrol* station

2801   train/railway* station

2802   statue

2803   Stay there!

Steak is a cut of meat.
2804   steak

2805   to steal

2806   steam

2807   Kinves are made of steel.

2808   steep

2809   steer/bullock*

2811   stem

2812   step

She stepped in the puddle.
2813   to step in

2810   to steer

Dad made stew for dinner.
2815   stew

2816   stick

2814   to step out

Bud's hands are all sticky.
2817   sticky

Uncle Joe has a stiff leg.

Can you keep a stiff upper lip?

2818   stiff

It really stings.
2819   to sting

A bee sting
2820   sting

Skunks stink.
2821   to stink

Stir it before you taste it!

2822   to **stir**

2823   **stockings**

2824   to **stoke**

2825   **stomach**

Throwing **stones** is dangerous.

2826   **stone**

The spider will land on the **stool**.

2827   **stool**

She **stoops** to get the ball.

2828   to **stoop/bend down***

2829   **stop**

2832   **store/shop***

Is this the **stork** that brought Ashley?

2833   **stork**

2834   **storm**

2830   He **stops** the train.

Aunt Sally reads a **story**.

2835   **story**

2836   **stove/cooker***

2837   **straight**

2831   to **stop over**

2838   to **strain**

2839   to **strain**

A very **strange** animal

2840   **strange**

Jim got too close and the ape is **strangling** him.

2841   to **strangle**

| 2842 | strap | 2843 | straw | 2844 | strawberry | 2845 | stream |

2846   streamer/pennant*   2847   street   2848   street light/lamp*   How far can she **stretch** it?   2849   to **stretch**

2850   stretcher   The workers are on **strike** for more money.   2851   strike   It is not nice to **strike** people.   2852   to **strike**   2853   string

Lots of **stripes**   2854   stripe   2855   strong   2856   student   2857   to **study**

2858   a **stuffed** animal   2859   stump   A **submarine** travels underwater.   2860   submarine   2861   to **subtract**

2862 to suck	**Suddenly,** it began to rain. Pamela left **suddenly**. **2863** suddenly	Too much **sugar** is bad for you. **2864** sugar	**2865** suit
2866 suitcase	**2867** summer	**2868** sun	**Sunday** is the day between Saturday and Monday. **2869** Sunday
The **sundial** tells the time. **2870** sundial	The **sunflower** always faces the sun. **2871** sunflower	**2872** sunrise	**2873** sunset
We shop at the **supermarket**. **2874** supermarket	**2875** supper/dinner*	I am **sure** tomorrow will be a sunny day. Ashley will go tomorrow for **sure**. That is a **sure** way to win. **2876** sure	The **surface** of the moon is pitted with craters. **2877** surface
2878 surgeon	My first name is Ashley and my **surname** is Potter. **2879** surname	They didn't tell Ashley beforehand. **2880** surprise party	I give myself up! **2881** to surrender

They have **surrounded** him.

2882   to **surround**

2883   suspenders/braces*

2884   to **swallow**

2885   **swan**

2886   to **swap**

A **swarm** of angry bees

2887   **swarm**

It gets very hot in the sauna.

2888   to **sweat**

2889   **sweater/sweatshirt***

2890   to **sweep**

2891   **sweet**

The car **swerved** to miss the cat.

2892   to **swerve**

Gerry can **swim** like a fish.

2893   to **swim**

2894   **swing**

2895   to **swing**

2896   **switch**

Switch on the light, please.

It is best to **switch** off the television.

2897   to **switch**

2898   to **swoop**

2899   **sword**

2900   **sycamore**

Pancakes and maple **syrup**

2901   **syrup**

The mug is on the **table**.

2902   table

2903   tablecloth

2904   tablet

2905   tack

Ashley must **tackle** that problem soon.

Al **tackled** Hector during the football game.

2906   to tackle

Tadpoles become frogs.

2907   tadpole

2908   tail

2910   to take

2911   to take apart

2912   to take away

2913   to take back

2914   to take off

2915   to take off

2916   to take out

2917   take-out/take-away*

2909   tailor

Sylvia tells a long **tale** to Ashley

2918   tale

Ashley and Sylvia are in the **talent** show.

Sylvia has a great **talent** for acting.

2919   talent

It is Ashley's turn to **talk**.

2920   to talk

2921 tall	2922 tambourine

Circus lions are **tame.**

2923 tame	2924 tan
2925 tangerine	2926 tangled
2927 tank	2928 tanker

This **tap** drips.

2929 tap	2930 tape
2931 to tape	2932 tape recorder
2933 tar	2934 target
2935 tarragon	2936 tart

His **task** is to sweep the floor.

This is very **tasty** food, I am enjoying it a lot.

2937 task	2938 to taste
2939 tasty	2940 taxi

2941   a cup of **tea**

Miss Parker **teaches** us at school.

2942   to **teach**

She is our **teacher**.

2943   **teacher**

All on the same **team**

2944   **team**

2945   **teapot**

2946   **tear**

2947   to **tear**

Never **tear out** a page!

2948   to **tear out**

This **telegram** contains urgent news.

2949   **telegram**

2950   **telephone**

2951   to **telephone**

2952   **telescope**

Also called **telly** for short

2953   **television**

Guess what I heard!

2954   to **tell**

Grover has a bad **temper**.

He cannot control his **temper**.

2955   **temper**

2956   **temperature**

2957   **ten** apples

2958   **tennis** racquet and ball

2959   **tennis** shoe

Ashley has slept in a **tent**.

2960   **tent**

2961 tenth	A computer **terminal** 2962 terminal	2963 to **test** the water	2964 to **thank**
The ground **thaws** in the spring. 2965 to thaw	2966 theater/theatre*	2967 there	2968 thermometer
2969 thick	A **thief** is also called a robber. 2970 thief	2971 thigh	2972 thimble
2973 thin	A person is not a **thing**. Ashley says many funny **things**. 2974 thing	2975 to think	2976 third
2977 thirsty	2978 thistle	**Thorns** can hurt. 2979 thorn	2980 thread

Ashley can only **thread** a large needle.

2981   to thread

2982   three

2983   threshold

2984   throat

The **throne** of the Queen

2985   throne

2986   to throw

2987 to throw up/be sick*

2988   thumb

A loud clap of **thunder**

2989   thunder

2990   thunderstorm

Thursday is the fifth day of the week.

Ashley goes to her swimming lesson on **Thursdays**.

2991   Thursday

2992   thyme

2993   ticket

2994   to tickle

At least one of them is **tidy**!

2995   tidy

I can fasten my own **tie**.

2996   tie

2998   tiger

2999   to tighten

3000   tiles

2997   to tie

The boat is **tilting** dangerously.

3001   to **tilt**

3002   What **time** is it?

3003   tiny

The boat has **tipped** over.

3004   to **tip**

3006   tiptoe

Our car needs new **tyres**.

3007   tire/tyre*

3008   tired

3005   to **tip**

3009   toad

Toast and jam

3010   toast

3011   toaster

School starts **today**.

Today is Mothers' Day.

Do your homework **today**!

3012   today

3013   toes

3014 We are sitting **together**.

3015   toilet

3016   tomato

Someone is buried in this **tomb**.

3017   tomb

Tomorrow is another day.

Àshley is going to see the dinosaurs at the museum **tomorrow**.

3018   tomorrow

3019   tongs

It is very rude to stick out your **tongue**.

3020   tongue

3021 It weighs a **ton.**

3022 tonsils

3023 tools

3024 tooth

3025 toothache

3026 toothbrush

3027 toothpaste

3028 top

The blocks **toppled** over.

3030 to **topple**

The Olympic **torch**

3031 torch

3032 tornado

The **top** is spinning.

3029 top

After the storm, the river flowed in a **torrent.**

3033 torrent

3034 tortoise

Cal **tosses** the ball to Sue.

3035 to **toss**

3036 to **touch**

3037 I am **tough.**

3038 to **tow**

Ashley's **towel** is wet.

3039 towel

The world's tallest **tower**

3040 tower

This **town** is near Ashley's home.

3041   town

Pick up your **toys**, please!

3042   toys

3043   to trace

3044   track

3045   tractor

3046   to trade

Bumper to bumper **traffic**

3047   traffic

3048   traffic light

The rustlers left a **trail** of hoofprints.

3049   trail

There is a horse in the **trailer**.

3050   trailer

3051   train

She **trained** Spot well.

3052   to train

3053   tramp

Do not **trample** the flowers!

3054   to trample

3055   trampoline

The glass is **transparent**.

3056   transparent

3057   to transport

3058   transporter/lorry*

3059   trap

3060   trapeze

Aunt Vera takes a lot of luggage when she **travels**.

3061 to **travel**

A **tray** full of drinks

3062 **tray**

3063 **tread**

3064 **treasure**

3065 **tree**

Judith **trembles** with fear.

3066 to **tremble**

3067 **trench**

3068 **trial**

A **triangle** has three sides.

3069 **triangle**

3070 **trick**

The water **trickles** down.

3071 to **trickle**

3072 **tricycle**

3073 **trigger**

3074 to **trim**

3075 a short **trip**

3076 to **trip**

3077 **trolley bus**

Colts like to **trot** and to gallop.

3078 to **trot**

3079 **trough**

3080 **trousers**

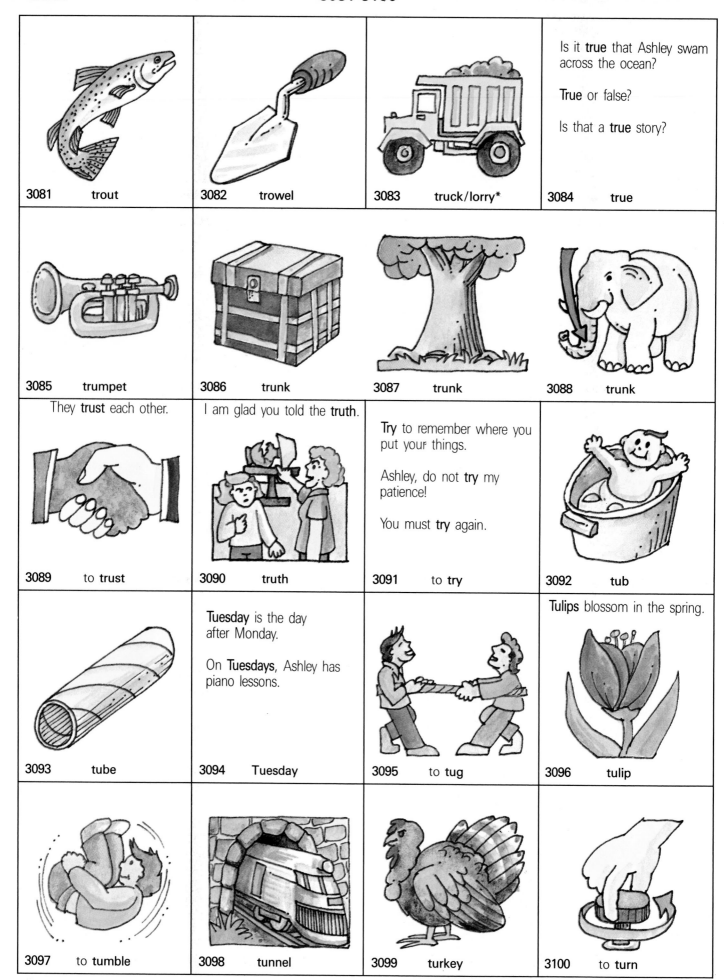

3081   trout

3082   trowel

3083   truck/lorry*

Is it **true** that Ashley swam across the ocean?

True or false?

Is that a **true** story?

3084   true

3085   trumpet

3086   trunk

3087   trunk

3088   trunk

They **trust** each other.

3089   to **trust**

I am glad you told the **truth**.

3090   truth

Try to remember where you put your things.

Ashley, do not **try** my patience!

You must **try** again.

3091   to **try**

3092   tub

3093   tube

Tuesday is the day after Monday.

On **Tuesdays**, Ashley has piano lessons.

3094   Tuesday

3095   to **tug**

Tulips blossom in the spring.

3096   tulip

3097   to **tumble**

3098   tunnel

3099   turkey

3100   to **turn**

3101 to turn off

3102 to turn on

Chuck **turned out** to be a bad boy.

Things **turned out** well.

3103 to turn out

Cheryl **turns over** the steak.

3104 to turn over

3105 turnip

3106 turntable

3107 turquoise

3108 turret

3109 turtle

3110 tusk

3111 tweezers

Ashley has been to the zoo **twice**.

Curtis has **twice** as many books as me.

3112 twice

There is a leaf on the **twig**.

3113 twig

3114 twins

Stars **twinkle**.

3115

3116 to twirl

3117 to twist

3118 two

Dad **types** all day.

3119 to type

3120 typewriter

	She is **ugly** but kind.		My **uncle** is my mother's brother. My other **uncle** is my father's brother.
	3121 ugly	3122 umbrella	3123 uncle

I am not going **under** any circumstances.

Ashley is hiding **under** the covers.

Children **under** 5 cannot go.

3124 under	3125 to understand	3126 underwear	3127 to undress

Harry **understands** the meaning of life.

3128 unhappy	3129 unicorn	3130 uniform	3131 university

Unicorns appear in fables.

Uncle Rick wears a **uniform**.

Antonia was a good student at **university**.

3132 to unload	3133 to unlock	3134 to unwrap	3135 upright

3136 upside-down	3137 to use	3138 to use up	3139 useful

Mum **uses** pepper for cooking.

She has **used up** all the pepper.

A very **useful** pocket knife

A **holiday** in the sun

3140   vacation/holiday*

3141   vapor/vapour*

Jim **varnishes** the wood to protect it.

3142   to varnish

3143   vase

3144   veal

There are hundreds of tasty **vegetables.**

3145   vegetable

A motor **vehicle**

3146   vehicle

Pat wears a **veil** over her face.

3147   veil

Veins carry blood back to your heart.

3148   vein

Venom is the poison found in some snakes.

Some insects also have **venom.**

3149   venom

A straight line up and down is **vertical.**

3150   vertical

Ashley thinks her brother Carl is **very** clever.

Very soon the soup will be ready.

Spot is a **very** nice dog.

3151   very

3152   vest/waistcoat*

We take our sick animals to the **vet.**

3153   veterinarian/veterinary surgeon*

The **victim** of a crime

3154   victim

Some people call it a VCR.

3155   video recorder

This is not how you use a **video tape**.

3156   video tape

When Emily and Ashley went camping, they had a nice **view** from the top of the mountain.

We each have our own point of **view.**

3157   view

3158   village

3159 villain

Grapes grow on a **vine.**

3160 vine

Ashley likes **vinegar** on her chips.

3161 vinegar

3162 violet

3163 violin

You need a **visa** to travel abroad.

3164 visa

There are many clouds tonight and the stars are barely **visible.**

The invisible man is not **visible** at all.

3165 visible

Roy **visits** his sick aunt.

3166 to visit

3167 visor

Someone who has a good **vocabulary** knows many words.

A good **vocabulary** is very important.

This dictionary helps increase your **vocabulary.**

3168 vocabulary

You can use your **voice** to sing.

3169 voice

3170 volcano

3171 volleyball

3172 volunteer

3173 to vomit

People **vote** to choose the Prime Minister.

3174 to vote

3175 voter

A, E, I, O, and U are the only **vowels** in the alphabet.

3176 vowel

A long sea **voyage**

3177 voyage

3178 vulture

Bert **wades** right in.

3179   to **wade**

3180   **waffle**

3181   **wagon/cart***

3182   to **wail**

3183   **waist**

Carole **waits** for the bus.

3184   to **wait**

Mum **wakes** him up.

3185   to **wake**

3186   to **walk**

3187   **wall**

3188   **wallet**

3189   **walnut**

3190   **walrus**

A magic **wand**

3191   **wand**

Ernest **wanders** freely round the countryside.

3192   to **wander**

Who **wants** more cereal?

Dad **wants** Ashley to help with the washing up.

She **wants** to help but there is no water.

3193   to **want**

Ashley hates **war.**

3194   **war**

3195   **wardrobe**

All sorts of things are stored in this **warehouse.**

3196   **warehouse**

A jumper and gloves should keep anyone **warm.**

3197   **warm**

It is nice to **warm up** by the fire.

3198 to **warm up**

3199 to **warn**

A rabbit **warren**

3200 **warren**

3201 **warrior**

3202 **wart**

3203 to **wash up**

3204 **washing machine**

3205 **washroom/toilet***

Ashley was stung by a **wasp**.

3206 **wasp**

He is **wasting** good food.

3207 to **waste**

A pocket **watch**

3208 **watch**

3209 to **watch**

3210 **water**

3211 **watering can**

3212 **watercress**

Over the **waterfall** in a barrel

3213 **waterfall**

3214 **watermelon**

3215 **waterproof**

3216 **waterskiing**

3217 **wave**

Kay **waves** to her friends.

3218   to **wave**

She has **wavy** hair.

3219   **wavy**

Candles are made from **wax.**

3220   **wax**

Mel is not as strong as his brothers.

3221   **weak**

Weapons are dangerous.

3222   **weapon**

Fred **wears** a hat and gloves with his coat.

3223   to **wear**

3224   **weasel**

What is the **weather** like?

3225   **weather**

3226   to **weave**

3227   **web foot**

3228   **wedding**

3229   **wedge**

Wednesday is the middle of the week.

On **Wednesdays**, Ashley takes out the rubbish.

3230   **Wednesday**

There is a **weed** in the garden.

3231   **weed**

Each **week** has seven days.

3232   **week**

Aunt Vera will visit us this **weekend**.

Saturday and Sunday make a **weekend**.

The weather forecast says it will rain this **weekend**.

3233   **weekend**

He **weeps** because he is sad.

3234   to **weep**

3235   to **weigh**

This picture is **weird**!

3236   **weird**

Kimberly **welcomes** her friend into the house.

3237   to **welcome**

3238   well

3239   I feel **well**.

West is to the left when North is up.

3240   west

3241   wet

3243   whale

3244   wharf

What has happened to Tigger's fur?

Ashley, **what** did you do to your cat?

What is it with you?.

3245   what

3242   to **wet**

3246   wheat

3247   wheel

3248   wheelbarrow

3249   wheelchair

When is Aunt Vera coming, Dad?

When the weekend starts.

When is that?

3250   when

We are lost and Mum has no idea **where** we are.

Where is the map?

I know **where** it is but I cannot find it.

3251   where

3252   which one

3253   to whine

3254   whip

3255   whippoorwill

3256   whisk

Cats have **whiskers**.

3257   whisker

Ashley **whispers** in her friend's ear.

3258   to **whisper**

3259   **whistle**

3260   to **whistle**

3261   **white**

3262   **Who** is going?

I want to know **why** Ashley took my tie.

Why can she not remember?

3263   **why**

The **wick** burns slowly.

3264   **wick**

3265   **wicked**

3266   **wide**

Mrs. Johnson is Mr. Johnson's **wife**.

3267   **wife**

3268   The lion is a **wild** animal.

3269   **willow**

Flowers **wilt** if you forget to water them.

3270   to **wilt**

3271   **wily**

3272   to **win**

Herb **winced** with pain.

3273   to **wince**

3274   **wind**

Wind it up!

3275   to **wind**

3276   **windbreaker**

3277   **windmill**

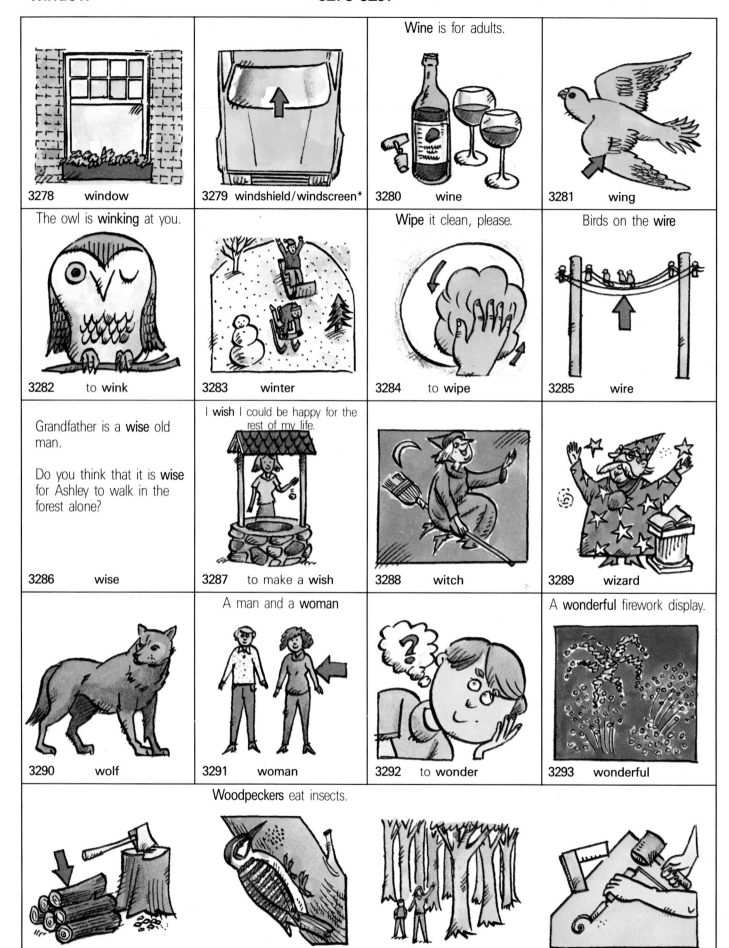

3278 window

3279 windshield/windscreen*

Wine is for adults.

3280 wine

3281 wing

The owl is **winking** at you.

3282 to wink

3283 winter

Wipe it clean, please.

3284 to wipe

Birds on the **wire**

3285 wire

Grandfather is a **wise** old man.

Do you think that it is **wise** for Ashley to walk in the forest alone?

3286 wise

I **wish** I could be happy for the rest of my life.

3287 to make a wish

3288 witch

3289 wizard

A man and a **woman**

3290 wolf

3291 woman

3292 to wonder

A **wonderful** firework display.

3293 wonderful

Woodpeckers eat insects.

3294 wood

3295 woodpecker

3296 woods

3297 woodwork

3298   wool

He said a strange **word**.

GLÜRP

3299   word

There are many different kinds of **work**.

3300   work

3301   to **work**

3303   workshop

3304   world

3305   worm

3302   to **work** out

Mum sometimes **worries** about Ashley.

3306   to **worry**

3307   wound

3308   to **wrap**

A flower **wreath**

3309   wreath

3310   wreck

3311   wren

3312   to **wrestle**

3313   to **wring**

3314   wrist

3315   wristwatch

3316   to **write**

I think our bus is going the **wrong** way.

It is **wrong** to cheat and to lie.

Are they **wrong** about this?

3317   wrong

3318 X-ray

3319 xylophone

A rather small **yacht**

3320 yacht

We have a nice garden.

3321 yard/garden*

Monty **yawns** when he is very tired.

3322 to yawn

Another **year**

3323 year

3324 to yell

3325 yellow

Yes Virginia, there is a Santa Claus.

Is it **yes**, is it no, or is it maybe?

If you say **yes**, you had better be sure.

3326 yes

Yesterday Ashley was sick from eating too much ice cream.

What did you do **yesterday**?

3327 yesterday

3328 to yield/give way*

An egg **yolk**

3329 yolk

3330 young

Ashley drew this **zebra**.

3331 zebra

3332 zero

3333 zipper/zip*

3334 zoo

3335 to zoom

This is my last word.

3336 zucchini/courgette*

a

abacus 1
about 2
above 3
absent 4
accelerator 5, 1111
accent 6
accident 7
accordion 8
accuse (to) 9
ace 10
ache (to) 11
acid 12
acorn 13
acrobat 14
across 15
add (to) 16
address 17
admiral 18
adore (to) 19
adult 20
advance (to) 21
advantage 22
adventure 23
aeroplane 39
afraid (to be) 24
Africa 25
after 26
afternoon 27
afters 2273
again 28
against 29
age 30
agile 31
aground 32
ahead 33
aid 34
aim (to) 35
air 36
air mattress 37
airtight 38
airplane 39
airport 40
aisle 41
alarm clock 42
album 43
alight 44
alive 45
all 46

alley 47
alligator 48
almond 49
almost 50
alone 51
along 52
aloud 53
alphabet 54
already 55
alright (to be) 56
also 57
aluminium 58
aluminum 58
always 59
ambulance 60
among 61
anchor 62
ancient 63
angle 64
angry (to be) 65
animals 66
ankle 67
announce (to) 68
another 69
answer 70
ant 71
Antarctic 72
antelope 73
antlers 74
any 75
anything 76
anywhere 77
apart 78
ape 79
apiary 80
apologise (to) 81
apologize (to) 81
appear (to) 82, 2625
applaud (to) 83
apple 84
apple core 85
approach (to) 86
apricot 87
April 88
apron 89
aquarium 90
arch 91
architect 92
Arctic 93
argue (to) 94
arm 94

armchair 96
armor 97
armour 97
armpit 98
around 99
arrange (to) 100
arrest (to) 100
arrive (to) 102
arrow 103
artichoke 104
artist 105
as 106
ash 107
ashtray 108
Asia 109
ask (to) 110
asleep 111
asparagus 112
aspirin 113
astonish (to) 114
astronaut 115, 633
astronomer 116
at 117
athlete 118
atlas 119
atmosphere 120
atom 121
attach (to) 122
attention 123
attic 124
aubergine 877
audience 125
August 126
aunt 127
Australia 128
author 129
automatic 130
autumn 131, 945
avalanche 132
avocado 133
awake 134
away (to be) 135
awful 136
awkward 137
axe 138
axle 139

b

baby 140
baby carriage 141
back 142
back up (to) 143
bacon 144
bad 145
badge 146
bag 147
bait 148
bake (to) 149
baker 150
bakery 151
balance 152
balcony 153
bald 154
ball 155
ballerina 156
ballet 157
balloon 158, 159
banana 160
band 161, 162
bandage 163
bang (to) 164
banger 1000
banister 165, 2335
bank 166
banknote 247
bar 167, 168
barbed wire 169
barber 170
bare 171
bargain 172
barge 173
bark (to) 174
bark 175
barley 176
barn 177
barracks 178
barrel 179, 180
barrette 181
barrier 182
base 183, 184
baseball 185
basement 186
basil 187
basket 188
basketball 189
bat 190, 191

discuss (to) 781
disease 782
disguise 783
disgusting 1215
dish 784
dishonest 785
dishwater 786
dislike (to) 787
dissolve (to) 788
distance 789
distant 790
district 791
ditch 792
dive (to) 793
divide (to) 794
dizzy (to be) 795
do (to) 796
dock 797
doctor 798
dog 799
doll 800
dolphin 801
dome 802
donkey 803
door 804
doorknob 805
double 806
dough 807
dove 808
down 809
doze (to) 810
dozen 811
drag (to) 812
dragon 813
dragonfly 814
drain 815
draw (to) 816
drawbridge 817
drawer 818
dream 819
dream (to) 820
dress 821
dress (to) 822
dresser 823
dessmaker's
　　dummy 1056
dribble (to) 824
drift (to) 825
drill (to) 826
drill 827
drink 828

drink (to) 829
drip (to) 830
drive (to) 831
driver 832
drizzle 833
drool (to) 834
drop 835
drop (to) 836
drop in (to) 837
drop off (to) 838
drop out (to) 839
drowsy (to be) 840
drum 841
dry 842
dry (to) 843
dry cleaner 844
dryer 845
duchess 846
duck 847
duel 848
duke 849
dump 850
dump (to) 851
dumptruck 852
dungeon 853
dusk 854
dust 855
dust bin 1104
dwarf 856

e

each 857
eagle 858
ear 859
early 860
earn (to) 861
Earth 862
earth 863
earthquake 864
easel 865
east 866
easy 867
eat (to) 868
eat breakfast 869
eat lunch 870
eat dinner 871
echo 872
eclipse 873

edge 874
eel 875
egg 876
eggplant 877
eiderdown 2319
eight 878
eighth 879
elastic 880
elbow 881
election 882
electrician 883
electricity 884
elephant 885
elevator 886
elk 887
elm 888
embarrass (to) 889
embrace (to) 890
embroidery 891
emergency 892
empty 893
end 894
enemy 895
engine 896
engine driver 897
engineer 897
enjoy (to) 898
enormous 899
enough (to be) 900
enter (to) 901
entrance 902
envelope 903
equal 904
equator 905
errand 906
escalator 907
escape (to) 908
Europe 909
evaporation 910
even 911, 912
evergreen 913
every 914
exam 915
examine (to) 916
example 917
exclamation mark 918
excuse (to) 919
exercise (to) 920
exist (to) 921
exit (to) 922
expand (to) 923

expect (to) 924
expensive 925
experiment 926
expert 927
explain (to) 928
explore (to) 929
explosion 930
extinguisher 931
eye 932
eyebrow 933
eyeglasses 934
eyelash 935

f

fable 936
face 937
factory 938
fail (to) 939, 940
fair 941
fairy 942
faith 943
fake 944
fall 945
fall (to) 946
fall down (to) 947
fall off (to) 948
false 949
family 950
famous 951
fan 952
fancy 953
fang 954
far (to be) 955
farewell 956
farm 957
farmer 958
fast 959
fasten (to) 960
fat 961
fatal 962
father 963
faucet 964
fault 965
favor 966
favorite 967
favour 966
favourite 967
fear (to) 968

feast 969
feather 970
February 971
feed (to) 972
feel (to) 973
female 974
fence 975
fender 976
fern 977
ferry 978
festival 979
fever 980
few 981
field 982
fifth 983
fight (to) 984
file 985
fill (to) 986
fill up (to) 987
film 988, 1851
filthy 989
fin 990
fine 991, 992
finger 993
fingernail 1869
fingerprint 994
finish (to) 995
fir 996
fire 997
fire engine 998
fire escape 999
firecracker 1000
firefighter 1001
fireplace 1002
firm 1003
first 1004
first year 1177
fish 1005
fish (to) 1006
fishhook 1007
fist 1008
five 1009
fix (to) 1010
flag 1011
flake 1012
flame 1013
flap (to) 1014
flare 1015
flash 1016
flashlight 1017
flask 1018

flat 1019
flatten (to) 1020
flavor 1021
flavour 1021
flea 1022
flee (to) 1023
fleece 1024
flesh 1025
float (to) 1026
flock 1027
flood 1028
floor 1029
flour 1030
flow (to) 1031
flower 1032
flu 1033
fluff 1034
fluid 1035
fly 1036, 1037
fly (to) 1038
foam 1039
fog 1040
fold (to) 1041
follow (to) 1042
food 1043
foot 1044
football 1045
footprint 1046
footsteps 1047
for 1048
force (to) 1049
forehead 1050
forest 1051
forget (to) 1052
forgive (to) 1053
fork 1054
forklift 1055
form 1056, 1177
fort 1057
forward 1058
fossil 1059
foul 1060
foundation 1061
fountain 1062
fox 1063
fraction 1064
fragile 1065
frame 1066
freckle 1067
free 1068
freeze (to) 1069

French horn 1375
fresh 1070
Friday 1071
fridge 1072
friend 1073
frighten (to) 1074
frog 1075
from 1076
front 1077
frost 1078
frown (to) 1079
fruit 1080
fry (to) 1081
frying pan 1082
fuel 1083
full 1084
full stop 2087
fun 1085
fund 1086
funeral 1087
funnel 1088
funny 1089
fur 1090
furnace 1092
furniture 1093
furry 1091
fuse 1094

g

gale 1095
gallery 1096
gallop (to) 1097
game 1098
gander 1099
gang 1100
gaol 1476
gap 1101
garage 1102
garbage 1103
garbage can 1104
garden 1105, 3321
gargle (to) 1106
garlic 1107
garter 1108
gas 1109, 1110
gas pedal 1111
gas pump 1112
gas station 1113

gate 1114
gather (to) 1115
gears 1116
gem 1117
general 1118
generous 1119
gentle 1120
gentleman 1121
genuine 1122
geography 1123
geranium 1124
gerbil 1125
germ 1126
get (to) 1127
get back (to) 1130
get in (to) 1132
get off (to) 1131
get on (to) 1129
get rid of (to) 1128
get up (to) 1133
ghost 1134
giant 1135
gift 1136
gigantic 1137
giggle (to) 1138
gill 1139
ginger 1140
gingerbread 1141
gipsy 1142
giraffe 1143
girl 1144
give (to) 1145
give back (to) 1146
give up (to) 1147
give away (to) 3328
glacier 1148
glad (to be) 1149
glass 1150, 1151
glasses 1152
glide (to) 1153
glider 1154
gloves 1155
glue 1156
go (to) 1157
go down (to) 1158
go in (to) 1159
go up (to) 1160
goal 1161
goat 1162
goggles 1163
gold 1164

goldfish 1165
golf 1166
good 1167
goodbye 1168
goose 1169
gooseberry 1170
gorgeous 1171
gorilla 1172
govern (to) 1173
government 1174
grab (to) 1175
gracious (to be) 1176
grade 1177
grain 1178
gram 1179
grandchild 1180
grandfather 1181
grandmother 1182
granite 1183
grant (to) 1184
grape 1185
grapefruit 1186
graph 1187
grass 1188
grasshopper 1189
grater 1190
grave 1191
gravel 1192
gravity 1193
gravy 2506
graze (to) 1194
gray 1202
grease 1195
great 1196
greedy 1197
green 1198
green bean 1199
greenhouse 1200
greet (to) 1201
grey 1202
grill (to) 1203
grimy 1204
grin (to) 1205
grind (to) 1206
grip (to) 1207
groan (to) 1208
grocer 1209
groceries 1210
groom 1211, 1212
groom (to) 1213
groove 1214

gross 1215
ground 1216
groundhog 1217
group 1218
grow (to) 1219
growl (to) 1220
grown-up 1221
guard 606
guard (to) 1222
guess (to) 1223
guest 1224
guide (to) 1225
guilty 1226
guinea pig 1227
guitar 1228
gulf 1229
gull 1230
gum 1231, 1232
gutter 1233

h

habit 1234
haddock 1235
hail 1236
hair 1237
hairbrush 1238
hairdresser 1239
hairdryer 1240
hairgrip 299
hair slide 181
half 1241
hall 1242
Halloween 1243
Hallowe'en 1243
hallway 1244
halt (to) 1245
hammer 1246
hammer (to) 1247
hammock 1248
hamster 1249
hand 1250
handbag 2294
hand out (to) 1251
hand brake 1252
handcuffs 1253
handicap 1254
handkerchief 1264
handle 1255

handrail 1256
handsome 1257
handy 1258
hang (to) 1259
hang on (to) 1260
hang up (to) 1261
hangar 1262
hanger 1263
happen (to) 1265
happy (to be) 1266
harbor 1267
harbour 1267
hard 1268
hare 1269
harm (to) 1270
harmonica 1271
harness 1272
harp 1273
harsh 1274
harvest (to) 1275
hat 1276
hat-stand 2327
hatch (to) 1277
hatchet 1278
haul (to) 1279
haunted 1280
have (to) 1281
hawk 1282
hay 1283
haze 1284
hazel 1285
hazelnut 1286
head 1287
headband 161
headache 1288
headrest 1289
head teacher 2243
heal (to) 1290
healthy 1291
heap 1292
hear (to) 1293
heart 1294
heat (to) 1295
heater 1296
heave (to) 1297
heaven 1298
heavy 1299
hedge 1300
hedgehog 1301
heel 1302
helicopter 1303

hell 1304
hello 1305
helm 1306
helmet 1307
help (to) 1308
helpless 1309
hem 1310
hemisphere 1311
hen 1312
heptagon 1313
herbs 1314
herd 1515
here 1316
hermit 1317
hero 1318
heroine 1319
herring 1320
hesitate (to) 1321
hexagon 1322
hibernate (to) 1323
hiccough (to) 1324
hiccup (to) 1324
hide 1325
hide (to) 1326
hiding-place 1327
high 1328
high rise 1329
high school 1330
highway 1331
hijack (to) 1332
hill 1333
hinge 1334
hind 1335
hip 1336
hippopotamus 1337
history 1338
hit (to) 1339
hive 1340
hoard (to) 1341
hoarding 248
hoarse 1342
hobby 1343
hockey 1344
hockey puck 1345
hockey stick 1346
hoe 1347
hold (to) 1348
hold down (to) 1349
hole 1350
holiday 1351, 3140
hollow 1352

knock (to) 1545, 2343
knot 1546
know (to) 1547
knuckle 1548
koala bear 1549

l

label 1550
laboratory 1551
lace 1552
lace (to) 1553
ladder 1554
ladle 1555
lady 1556
ladybird 1557
ladybug 1557
ladyfingers 1558
lair 1559
lake 1560
lamb 1561
lame 1562
lamp 1563
lamp-post 1564
lance 1565
land 1566
land (to) 1567
landing 1568
landlord 1569
lane 1570
language 1571
lantern 1572
lap 1573
larch 1574
lard 1575
large 1576
lark 1577
lash 1578
last 1579
last (to) 1580
latch (to) 1581
late 1582
lather 1583
laugh (to) 1584
launch 1585
launch (to) 1586
launchpad 1587
laundry 1588, 1589
launderette 1589

lavender 1590
law 1591
lawn 1592
lawn mower 1593
lay (to) 1594
layer 1595
lazy (to be) 1596
lead 402, 1603
lead (to) 1597
leader 1598
leaf 1599
leak (to) 1600
lean (to) 1601
learn (to) 1602
leash 1603
leather 1604
leave (to) 922, 1605, 1606
ledge 1607
leek 1608
left 1609
left-handed 1610
leg 1611
legend 1612
lemon 1613
lemonade 1614
lend (to) 1615, 1674
lens 1616
leopard 1617
leotard 1618
less 1619
lesson 1620
let (to) 1621
letter 1622, 1623
lettuce 1624
level 1625
lever 1626
liar 1627
library 1628
licence 1629
lick (to) 1630
lid 1631
lie (to) 1632
lie down (to) 1633
life 1634
lifeboat 1635
lift 886
lift (to) 1636
light 1637
light (to) 1638
lightbulb 1639

lighten (to) 1640
lighthouse 1641
lightning 1642
lightning rod 1643
like (to) 1644
likely 1645
lilac 1646
lily 1647
limb (to) 1648
lime 1649
limit 1650
limp (to) 1651
line 1652
linen 1653
liner 1654
lining 1655
link (to) 1656
lint 1657
lion 1658
lips 1659
lipstick 1660
liquid 1661
list 1662
listen (to) 1663
liter 1664
litre 1664
litter (to) 1665
little 1666
live (to) 1667
lively 1668
living room 1669
lizard 1670
load (to) 1671, 1672
loaf 1673
loan (to) 1674
lobster 1675
lock (to) 1676
lock 1677
locomotive 1678
locust 1679
lodge 1680
loft 1681
log 1682
lollipop 1683
lonely 1684
long 1685
look (to) 1686
loom 1687
loop 1688
loose 1689
lorry 852, 3058, 3083

lose (to) 1690
lotion 1691
loud 1692
loudspeaker 1693
lounge 1669
lounge (to) 1694
love 1695
love (to) 1696
lovely 1697
low 1698
lower (to) 1699
lucky 1700
luggage 1701
lukewarm 1702
lullaby 1703
lumber 1704
lump 529, 1705
lunch 1706
lunchbox 1707
lung 1708

m

magazine 1709
maggot 1710
magic 1711T
magician 1712
magnet 1713
magnificient 1714
magnifying glass 1715
magpie 1716
mail (to) 1717
mail carrier 1718
maize 629
make (to) 1719
makeup 1720
male 1721
mallet 1722
man 1723
mandarin 1724
mandolin 1725
mane 1726
mango 1727
manners 1728
many 1729
map 1730
marble 1731
marbles 1732
march (to) 1733

March 1734
mare 1735
marigold 1736
mark (to) 1737
mark 1738
market 1739
marry (to) 1740
marsh 1741
mash (to) 1742
mask 1743
mass 1744
mast 1745
master (to) 1746
match 1747, 1748
mathematics 1749
matter 1750
mattress 1751
May 1752
maybe 1753
mayor 1754
maze 1755
meadow 1756
meadowlark 1757
meal 1758
mean 1759
measles 1760
measure (to) 1761
meat 1762
mechanic 1763
medal 1764
medicine 1765
medium 1766
meet (to) 1767
meeting 1768
megaphone 378
melon 1769
melt (to) 1770
member 1771
menu 1772
mercy 1773
mermaid 1774
merry 1775
mess 1776
message 1777
messenger 1778
metal 1779
meteorite 1780
meter 1781, 1782
metre 1782
method 1783
metronome 1784

microphone 1785
microscope 1786
microwave oven 1787
midday 1788
middle 1789
midget 1790
midnight 1791
mile 1792
milk 1793
mill 1794
milometer 1936
mind 1795
mine 1796
miner 1797
mineral 1798
minnow 1799
mint 1800
minus 1801
minute 1802
miracle 1803
mirage 1804
mirror 1805
miser 1806
miss (to) 1807
missile 1808
mist 1809
mistletoe 1810
mittens 1811
mix (to) 1812
mixer 1813
moat 1814
mock (to) 1815
mockingbird 1816
model 1817
modern 1818
moist 1819
mold 1842
mole 1820, 1821
moment 1822
Monday 1823
money 1824
monkey 1825
monkfish 1826
monster 1827
month 1828
monument 1829
mood 1830, 1831
moon 1832
moose 1833
morning 1834
mortar 1835

mosaic 1836
mosquito 1837
moss 1838
mother 1839
motor 1840
motorcycle 1841
motorway 1331
mould 1842
mound 1843
mount (to) 1844
mountain 1845
mouse 1846
moustache 1847
mouth 1848
move (to) 1849
movement 1850
movie 1851
mow (to) 1852
much 1853
mud 1854
mule 1855
multiply (to) 1856
mumps 1857
murder (to) 1858
muscle 1859
museum 1860
mushroom 1861
music 1862
musician 1863
mussel 1864
must 1865
mustache 1847
mustard 1866
muzzle 1867

n

nail 1868
fingernail 1869
nail clipper 1870
nail (to) 1871
naked 1872
name 1873
napkin 1874
nappy 760
narrow 1875
nation 1876
natural 1877
nature 1878

naughty (to be) 1879
navigate (to) 1880
near 1881
neat 1882
necessary 1883
neck 1884
necklace 1885
nectar 1886
nectarine 1887
need 1888
need (to) 1889
needle 1890
neglect (to) 1891
neigh (to) 1892
neighbor 1893
neighbour 1893
neither 1894
neon sign 1895
nephew 1896
nerve 1897
nervous 1898
nest 1899
nettle 1900
never 1901
new 1902
news 1903
newspaper 1904
next 1905
nibble (to) 1906
nice 1907
nickel 1908
nickname 1909
niece 1910
night 1911
nightingale 1912
nightmare 1913
nine 1914
ninth 1915
no 1916
noble 1917
nobleman 1918
nobody 1919
noise 1920
noon 1921
north 1922
nose 1923
number plate 1629
nut 1924
nutcracker 1925
nylon 1926

o

oak 1927
oar 1928
oasis 1929
oblong 1930
observe (to) 1931
ocean 1932
octagon 1933
October 1934
octopus 1935
odometer 1936
odor 1937
odour 1937
off 1938
offer (to) 1939
officer 1940
often 1941
oil 1942
ointment 1943
old 1944
olive 1945
omelette 1946
on 1947
once 1948
one 1949
onion 1950
only 1951
open 1952
open (to) 1953
operation 1954
opossum 1955
opposite 1956
or 1957
orange 1958, 1959
orchard 1960
orchestra 1961
orchid 1962
order (to) 1963
oregano 1964
organ 1965
oriole 1966
orphan 1967
ostrich 1968
otter 1969
ounce 1970
outdoors 1971
outfit 1972
oval 1973
oven 1974

overboard 1975
overcoat 1976
overflow (to) 1977
overshoe 1978
overturn (to) 1979
owe (to) 1980
owl 1981
own (to) 1982
ox 1983
oxygen 1984
oyster 1985

p

pack (to) 1986
package 1987
pad 1988, 1989
paddle 1990
paddle (to) 1991
padlock 1992
page 1993
pail 1994
pain 1995
paint 1996, 1997
paint (to) 1998
paintbrush 1999
painter 2000
painting 2001
pair 2002
pajamas 2302
palace 2003
pale 2004
palette 2005
palm 2006
pan 2007
pancake 2008
panda 2009
panel 2010
panpipe 2011
pansy 2012
pant (to) 2013
panther 2014
pants 2015
papaya 2016
paper 2017
parachute 2018
parade 2019
parallel lines 2020
paralysed 2021

paralyzed 2021
parcel 2022
parent 2023
park 2024
park (to) 2025
parka 2026
parliament 2027
parrot 2028
parsley 2029
parsnip 2030
particle 2031
partner 2032
party 2033
pass (to) 2034
pass out (to) 2035
passage 2036
passenger 2037
passport 2038
past 2039
pasta 2040
paste (to) 2041
pastime 2042
pastry 2043
pasture 2044
patch 2045
path 2046
patient (to be) 2047
patient 2048
pattern 2049
pause (to) 2050
pavement 2051
paw 2052
pay (to) 2053
pay phone 2054
peace 2055
peach 2056
peacock 2057
peak 2058
peal 2059
peanut 2060
pear 2061
pearl 2062
peas 2063
peat 2064
pebble 2065
pecan 2066
peck (to) 2067
pedal 2068
pedal (to) 2069
pedestrian 2070

pedestrian crossing 2071
peel (to) 2072
pelican 2073
pen 2074
pencil 2075
pendulum 2076
penguin 2077
penknife 2078
pennant 2846
pentagon 2079
people 2080
pepper 2081
peppermint 2082
perch 2083, 2084
performance 2085
perfume 2086
period 2087
periwinkle 2088
person 2089
pest 2090
pester (to) 2091
pet 2092
pet (to) 2093
petal 2094
petrol 1110
petrol pump 1112
petunia 2095
pharmacist 2096
pharmacy 2097
pheasant 2098
phone 2099
phone (to) 411
phone box 2054, 2272
photograph 2100
piano 2101
pick (to) 2102
pick up (to) 2103
pickaxe 2104
pickles 2105
pickle (to) 2106
picnic 2107
picture 2108
pie 2109
piece 2110
piece (to) 2111
pier 2112
pig 2113
pigeon 2114
pigsty 2115
pile 1292, 2116

q

sap 2501
sardine 2502
satellite 2503
satin 2504
Saturday 2505
sauce 2506
sausage 2507
save (to) 2508
saw 2509
saw (to) 2510
sawdust 2511
say (to) 2512
scaffolding 2513
scald (to) 2514
scale 2515
scallop 2516
scalp 2517
scar 2518
scare (to) 2519
scarecrow 2520
scarf 2521
scarlet 2522
scene 2523
scenery 2524
scholarship 2525
school 2526
schooner 2527
scissors 2528
scoop (to) 2529
scooter 2530
scorched 2531
score (to) 2532
scout 2533
scrap 2534
scrape (to) 2535
scraper 2536
scratch 237
screen 2538
screw 2539
screwdriver 2540
scrub (to) 2541
sculptor 2542
seahorse 2543
sea 2544
seagull 2545
seal 2546
seam 2547
search (to) 2548
searchlight 2549
season 2550
seat 2551

seatbelt 2552
seaweed 2553
second 2554
secondary
   school 1330
secret 2555
see (to) 2556
see-saw 2557
seed 2558
seem (to) 2559
seize (to) 2560
selfish (to be) 2561
sell (to) 2562
semicircle 2563
send (to) 2564
sensitive 2565
sentence 2566
sentry 2567
September 2568
serve (to) 2569
serviette 1874
seven 2570
seventh 2571
several 2572
sew (to) 2573
sewing machine 2574
shabby 2575
shack 2576
shadow 2577
shaggy 2578
shake (to) 2579
shallow 2580
shampoo 2581
share (to) 2582
shark 2583
sharp 2584
sharpener 2585,
   2586, 2587
shatter (to) 2588
shave (to) 2589
shears 2590
sheath 2591
sheep 2592
sheet 2593
shelf 2594
shell 2595
shelter 2596
shepherd 2597
shield 2598
shin 2599
shine (to) 2600

shingle 2601
shingles 2602
shiny 2603
ship 2604
shipwreck 2605
shirt 2606
shiver (to) 2607
shock 2608
shoes 2609
shoelace 2610
shoemaker 2611
shoot (to) 2612
shop 2613, 2832
shopkeeper 2614
shop window 2615
shore 2616
short 2617
shorts 2618
shoulder 2619
shout (to) 2620
shove (to) 2621
shovel 2622
show (to) 2623
show off (to) 2624
show up (to) 2625
shower 2626
shriek (to) 2627
shrimp 2628
shrink (to) 2629
shrub 2630
shuffle (to) 2631
shutters 2632
shy 2633
sick 2634
sick (to be) 2987
side 2635
sideboard 1409
sidewalk 2636
sigh (to) 2637
sign 2638
signal (to) 2639
signature 2640
silent 2641
sill 2642
silly 2643
silver 2644
simple 2645
sing (to) 2646
singular 2647
sink 2648
sink (to) 2649

sip (to) 2650
siren 2651
sister 2652
sit (to) 2653
six 2654
sixth 2655
size 2656
skate (to) 2657
skateboard 2658
skeleton 2659
sketch 2660
ski 2661
ski (to) 2662
skid (to) 2663
skin 2664
skip (to) 2665
skipper 2666
skirt 2667
skull 2668
sky 2669
skylark 2670
skyscraper 2671
slam (to) 2672
slanting 2673
slap (to) 2674
slash (to) 2675
slate 2676
sled 2677
sleep (to) 2678
sleeping bag 2679
sleepy 2680
sleet 2681
sleeve 2682
sleigh 2677
slice 2110
slide 2683
slim 2684
slimy 2685
sling 2686
slingshot 2687
slip (to) 2688
slipper 2689
slippery 2690
slob 2691
slope 2692
slot 2693
slouch (to) 2694
slow down (to) 2695
slush 2696
small 2697
smart 2698

smash (to) 2699
smear (to) 2700
smell (to) 2701
smelly 2702
smoke (to) 2703
smooth 2704
snack (to have) 2705
snail 2706
snake 2707
snap (to) 2708
sneakers 2709
sneeze (to) 2710
snooker 249
snorkel 2711
snow 2712
snowflake 2713
snowshoes 2714
soap 2715
soccer 2716
sock 2717
socket 2718
sofa 637, 2719
soft 2720
soldier 2721
sole 2722
solve (to) 2723
somersault (to) 2724
son 2725
song 2726
soon 2727
sorcerer 2728
sore (to be) 2729
sorrel 2730
sorry 2731
sort (to) 2732
soup 2733
sour 2734
south 2735
sow 2736
sow (to) 2737
spaceship 2738
spade 2739
spank (to) 2740
spare tire 2741
spare tyre 2741
spark 2742
sparkle (to) 2743
sparrow 2744
speak (to) 2745
spear 2746
spectacles 934

speed up (to) 2747
spell (to) 2748
spend (to) 2749
sphere 2750
spicy 2751
spider 2752
spike 2753
spill (to) 2754
spin (to) 2755
spinach 2756
spine 2757
spiral 2758
spire 2759
spit (to) 2760
splash (to) 2761
splinter 2762
spoiled 2763
sponge 2764
spool 2765
spoon 2766
spot 2767
spout 2768
sprain (to) 2769
spray (to) 2770
spread (to) 2771
spring 2772, 2773,
  2774
sprinkle (to) 2775
sprint (to) 2776
spruce 2777
square 2778
squash 2779
squat (to) 2780
squeeze (to) 2781
squid 2782
squirrel 2783
squirt (to) 2784
stable 2785
stage 2786
stain 2787
staircase 2788
stake 2789
stale 2790
stalk 2791
stallion 2792
stamp 2793
stand (to) 2794
star 2795
stare (to) 2796
starling 2797
start (to) 2798

starve (to) 2799
station 2800, 2801
statue 2802
stay (to) 2803
steak 2804
steal (to) 2805
steam 2806
steel 2807
steep 2808
steer 2809
steer (to) 2810
stem 2811
step 2812
step in (to) 2813
step out (to) 2814
stew 2815
stick 2816
sticky 2817
stiff 2818
sting (to) 2819
sting 2820
stink (to) 2821
stir (to) 2822
stockings 2823
stoke (to) 2824
stomach 2825
stone 2826
stool 2827
stoop 2828
stop 2829
stop (to) 2830
stop)over 2831
store 2832
stork 2833
storm 2834
story 2835
stove 2836
straight 2837
strain (to) 2838, 2839
strange 2840
strangle (to) 2841
strap 2842
straw 2843
strawberry 2844
stream 2845
streamer 2846
street 2847
street lamp 2848
street light 2848
stretch (to) 2849
stretcher 2850

strike 2851
strike (to) 2852
string 2853
stripe 2854
strong 2855
student 2856
study (to) 2857
stuff 2858
stump 2859
submarine 2860
subtract (to) 2861
suck (to) 2862
suddenly 2863
sugar 2864
suit 2865
suitcase 2866
summer 2867
sun 2868
Sunday 2869
sundial 2870
sunflower 2871
sunrise 2872
sunset 2873
supermarket 2874
supper 871, 2875
sure 2876
surface 2877
surgeon 2878
surname 2879
surprise 2880
surrender (to) 2881
surround (to) 2882
suspenders 2883
swallow (to) 2884
swan 2885
swap (to) 2886
swarm 2887
sweat (to) 2888
sweater 2279, 2889
sweatshirt 2889
sweep (to) 2890
sweet 712, 2891
sweets 423
swerve (to) 2892
swim (to) 2893
swing 2894
swing (to) 2895
switch 2896
switch (to) 2897
swoop (to) 2898
sword 2899

sycamore 2900
syrup 2901

table 2902
table lamp 1637
tablecloth 2903
tablet 2711, 2904
tack 2905
tackle (to) 2906
tadpole 2907
tail 2908
tailor 2909
take (to) 2910
take apart (to) 2911
take away 2917
take away (to) 2912
take back (to) 2913
take off (to) 2914,
    2915
take out (to) 2916
take-out 2917
tale 2918
talent 2919
talk (to) 2920
tall 2921
tambourine 2922
tame 2923
tan 2924
tangerine 2925
tangled 2926
tank 2927
tanker 2928
tap 964, 2929
tape 2930
tape (to) 2931
tape recorder 2932
tar 2933
target 2934
tarragon 2935
tart 2936
task 2937
taste (to) 2938
tasty 2939
taxicab 2940
tea 2941
teach (to) 2942
teacher 2943

team 2944
teapot 2945
tear 2946
tear (to) 2947
tear out (to) 2948
telegram 2949
telephone 2950
telephone (to) 2951
telescope 2952
television 2953
tell (to) 2954
temper 2955
temperature 2956
ten 2957
tennis 2958
tennis shoe 2959
tent 2960
tenth 2961
terminal 2962
test (to) 2963
thank (to) 2964
thaw (to) 2965
theater 2966
theatre 2966
there 2967
thermometer 2968
thick 2969
thief 2970
thigh 2971
thimble 2972
thin 2973
thing 2974
think (to) 2975
third 2976
thirsty 2977
thistle 2978
thorn 2979
thread 2980
thread (to) 2981
three 2982
threshold 2983
throat 2984
throne 2985
throw (to) 2986
throw up (to) 2987
thumb 2988
thunder 2989
thunderstorm 2990
Thursday 2991
thyme 2992
ticket 2993

tickle (to) 2994
tidy 2995
tie 2996
tie (to) 2997
tie up (to) 250
tiger 2998
tighten (to) 2999
tights 1926
tiles 3000
tilt (to) 3001
timber 1704
time 3002
tin opener 418
tiny 3003
tip (to) 3004, 3005
tiptoe (to) 3006
tire 3007
tired 3008
toad 3009
toast 3010
toaster 3011
today 3012
toe 3013
together 3014
toilet 3015, 3205
tomato 3016
tomb 3017
tomorrow 3018
tongs 3019
tongue 3020
ton 3021
tonsils 3022
tools 3023
tooth 3024
toothache 3025
toothbrush 3026
toothpaste 3027
top 3028, 3029
topple (to) 3030
torch 1017, 3031
tornado 3032
torrent 3033
tortoise 3034
toss (to) 3035
touch (to) 3036
tough (to be) 3037
tow (to) 3038
towel 3039
tower 3040
tower block 1329
town 3041

toys 3042
trace (to) 3043
track 3044
tractor 3045
trade (to) 3046
traffic 3047
traffic light 3048
trail 3049
trailer 3050
train 3051
train (to) 3052
trainers 2709
tramp 3053
trample (to) 3054
trampoline 3055
transparent 3056
transport (to) 3057
transporter 3058
trap 3059
trapeze 3060
travel (to) 3061
tray 3062
tread 3063
treasure 3064
tree 3065
tremble (to) 3066
trench 3067
trial 3068
triangle 3069
trick (to) 3070
trickle (to) 3071
tricycle 3072
trigger 3073
trim (to) 3074
trip 3075
trip (to) 3076
trolley bus 3077
trot (to) 3078
trough 3079
trousers 2015, 3080
trout 3081
trowel 3082
truck 3083
true 3084
trumpet 3085
trunk 3086, 3087,
    3088
trust (to) 3089
truth 3090
try (to) 3091
tub 3092

y

z

x